THE ARCHITECT

THE ARCHITECT

How to

START BUILDING

Your Family's Ecosystem

By

CONOR GALLAGHER

TAN Books
Gastonia, North Carolina

Cover & interior design by David Ferris, www.davidferrisdesign.com

ISBN: 978-1-5051-3628-9
Kindle ISBN: 978-1-5051-3664-7
ePUB ISBN: 978-1-5051-3663-0

Published in the United States by
TAN Books
PO Box 269
Gastonia, NC 28053

Printed in the United States of America

CONTENTS

INTRODUCTION

People always say to me, "How do you raise sixteen kids? I can barely manage two!" And my answer is, "I don't raise sixteen kids—I manage environments." They look at me with surprise, and then we have a fascinating conversation.

This little book is part of what I mean when I say, "I manage environments."

At some point in my parenting career, I realized a profound truth: no one was going to build the environment I wanted for my children other than me and my wife. I couldn't outsource this, as I could with much of our lives. I had to build something beautiful they could live in—and I don't mean a house. I mean a "home," yes, but a social life, a technologically safe life, an educational life, and so on. I was the architect, appointed by Almighty God, to design and build a life, an environment, or better yet, an ecosystem, that would produce virtuous and happy adults, who in turn would do the same thing for their own families.

My wife and I are the architects. And we hope to construct, with God's help, a masterpiece.

What are you building, dear reader? What is the environment you are constructing for your most important asset to reside in? Are you taking ownership of this eternally important project, or have you left it to the heathens of this world to construct on your behalf?

Are you the architect? Or are you not?

Read on and learn how to be one.

—Conor Gallagher

YOUR LIFE

IS THE FRUIT OF

YOUR OWN DOING

–JOSEPH CAMPBELL

CHAPTER 1

BE THE HERO, NOT THE VICTIM

The late American author and professor Joseph Campbell dedicated much of his career to studying and analyzing ancient literature and mythology. In his studies, he uncovered certain recurring patterns, ideas, and truths that lie at the heart of some of our most beloved stories and poems. But one quote that is particularly striking is about what it means to be a hero. Campbell wrote, "Your life is the fruit of your own doing. You have no one to blame but yourself." And elsewhere he wrote, "The big question is whether you're going to be able to say a hearty yes to your adventure."

Stories of myths and heroes have permeated our human identity since time out of mind. From epic poems and hieroglyphics to binge-worthy Netflix shows and comic books, we as a culture have long admired ordinary people placed in extraordinary situations. Our hearts race and we bray with elation when good triumphs over evil.

We long to be that hero. We long for the courage to overcome adversity and sorrow.

"Some are born great, some achieve greatness, and some have greatness thrust upon them."

–William Shakespeare

For the past fifty years or so, however, I would argue that we've buried such courage. We've sadly exchanged our role of aspiring to great virtue with self-pity. We've become self-made victims in a cruel world. But saddest of all is that this has become an accepted norm for many of us.

Now, what is this self-victimization? The simple definition is self-victimization is the tendency of individuals to perceive themselves as victims, attributing their problems and misfortunes to external factors rather than acknowledging their own responsibility. Why would someone want to do this? Because they desire sympathy, compassion, and frankly, a free hand out. They want someone to take the blame so they don't have to take responsibility for working hard, overcoming obstacles, and winning on their own merits. In our super-sensitive world, if you are a victim, others will take care of you. If you are a victim, you are entitled.

This cycle of self-made victims has become a virus within our culture. It's a psychological parasite that's spreading rampantly through this modern age. This isn't completely ridiculous though. In fact, it's quite understandable that this would happen in a culture filled with spoiled rotten brats. And remember: it doesn't take money to be spoiled rotten. My kids have grown up with plenty of money, but they are not spoiled in the least. (They have their issues but being spoiled ain't one of them.) With the number of kids in our family, they have been forced to work things out, to deny self, to help others when it is highly inconvenient. Even if you are poor, you have the ability to spoil your kids rotten by the way you raise them. We aren't talking money; we are talking how you raise your kids to be accountable for their own actions.

A story just from the other night may illustrate the point. We were watching the Yankees and Dodgers in the 4th game of the World Series. Imelda (12) went outside to get something from the refrigerator (the extra one) and a large glass bottle of sparkling water fell out of the fridge, shattering on the garage floor. A huge mess. Tons of little shards of glass. Water everywhere. She came inside and told me. I asked her if she was capable of cleaning up the mess or if she needed me. She said she could do it, albeit a little reluctantly, hoping I might take the burden from her. She asked her brother David (11) for help. He willingly left the game and helped her.

Now, I went outside to check on them three or four times and would have of course intervened if they needed help. But they handled it. They even moved the fridge in order to get the shards of glass that shattered beneath it. I saw little David pushing that fridge with his back, feet up against the water heater giving him leverage. It was a funny sight. It took at least thirty minutes, missing much of the game.

I think most parents would have done the clean up for them, or, had to force a much older sibling to help. I was so proud to see my kids handle such a big mess together. This, my friends, is why my kids end up being excellent employees: they know how to work. They are not the victims of a broken bottle. Rather, they were heroes that solved the problem.

Now, there are many factors and situations that can lead to true, justified victimization. True oppression exists. Real suffering can strike and leave families devastated and ruined. But most people in our culture live with all the modern comforts this century has to offer. Sturdy houses and apartments with running water and electricity; every new piece of technology; all the streaming services; the fastest internet; food that can be delivered at any moment....This is an age of instantaneous abundancy. Those that have it are sucked into it; those that don't have it long for it. It is a spoiled age obsessed with the material. It is a virtual age that despises the virtuous.

It's easy to imagine this spoiled brat on a micro level. You've seen it in movies, read it in novels, known some family that spoils their kids to death. That kid who has been spoiled is destined to see themselves as a victim of their circumstances. This is because they haven't had to persevere. They haven't had to fight through difficulty or truly yearn for something more. They simply complain about every meaningless frustration or things not going exactly as they wish.

My brother Brian makes this funny joke where he'll act like something's really wrong. I'll ask, "What's wrong, Brian?" He'll do this fake pouting cry and say, "My toaster doesn't have a bagel setting."

We have become self-made victims in many ways because our luxury cars don't pair with our smartphones, or our package won't arrive from Amazon instantly. We've lost sight of ourselves because we wallow in misfortune and blame others for it. We've shrugged off our great adventure and instead whine that we have to get off the couch.

YOU MUST BREAK THE CYCLE

The novelist G. Michael Hopf is credited with coining the saying, "Hard times create strong men. Strong men create good times. Good times create weak men. Weak men create hard times."

If you look back through American history (I'd argue back as far as the founding of any civilization) this has been humanity's cycle. It has been especially present in American culture since at least World War I.

Consider the generation that fought in World War I. The trench warfare was horrific and devastating. These young men came home from tragic battles and went to work, often very hard, manual labor jobs in factories, shipyards, or farms. They worked to build families and make lives after the war, and then the Great Depression struck. They didn't have any extended period of time of ease. These were hard times, to say the least. The Depression and post-war culture wreaked havoc in the country, but the people were tough, they persevered and never gave up.

The children that grew up in the Depression saw mom and dad fighting to have every little thing that they had. They learned to be grateful for what there was and work hard to get just a bit ahead. There was no room to become spoiled. These same children grew up and then went off to World War II themselves, already tough as nails from being Depression-era babies.

Those hard times in American society created strong men and women. They were strong from the Depression. They were strong from the war. They came back home, and wished to build strong lives, strong communities. They built factories and businesses. And through all of this, these strong men and women created good times.

As a result of their hard work, there came a boom in America. Throughout the 50s, 60s, and 70s, technology and industry soared. New homes were built, mass manufacturing made life easy and made necessities easily accessible.

But the next generation, the "baby boomers," disrupted much of this. My father is a quintessential baby boomer, born in 1950. When he turned 18 or 19 years old, what was going on in America? It was the sexual revolution. Woodstock and long hair. Suddenly, it's the anti-war movement, anti-patriotism, race wars. Some things improved, but many things began to fall apart, and major division entered society in unprecedented ways. The age of entitlement began.

MACRO CAUSES OF A VICTIM MINDSET

Mindsets changed in such drastic ways in a short amount of time. No longer was focus placed on family or communities or even a country, but instead it was shifted to the individual. JFK's famous line, "Ask not what your country can do for you, but what you can do for your country," was a prophetic warning of the upside-down mindset becoming prevalent. Ever since that baby boomer generation, the mindset has been "What can my country do for me?"

Advertising became aimed at the individual. Music and television provided narratives of self-centeredness. And at the same time, there was no longer worry or need to have a family or remain chaste, because the invention of "the pill" brought a new form of sexual freedom. Suddenly men and women become spoiled in a whole new way because there were no consequences to their sexual deviancy.

Babies became commodities. Families became customers. War became an industry because it was good for the economy.

So, in post-war America, these strong men and women made good times. My father's generation grew up in the good times, but those times created weak men and women.

Politically, this baby boomer generation embraced big government. With welfare and social programs holding over from the post-Depression years, what was supposed to be momentary relief for a devastated country became a foothold for power hungry politicians. The philosophy of the 60s was one of radical individualism. It should come as no surprise that a spirit of entitlement possessed our nation.

You can even see this weak-men-mentality manifesting itself in economic policy of "big government's going to have to take care of us." No longer was there a pride of place, of ownership, or community. Mindsets became "what can they do for *me*?"

MAKE YOUR KIDS CLEAN UP THE BROKEN GLASS

Those good times created these weak men and women. These weak men and women created an economic policy of entitlement and victimization. While welfare and social support for the poor is needed, big government used such programs to essentially victimize the populace, divide races, knowing that they could continually be put in office and elected when they promised to make things better and give things away. It became a game of weakening already weak people, promising to help but doing nothing in the end. And that dynamic is still going on politically and economically. Perhaps this was no better demonstrated than upon Barack Obama's election when people literally started asking, "Where's my new car?"

If you make the people weak, they will always need you. It's a constant circle of taking out legs from under people so that they must lean on someone else. Such a government and cultural zeitgeist becomes a tyrant, posing as savior.

> "No one can make you feel inferior without your consent."
> –*Eleanor Roosevelt*

This weak generation has been in charge for a long time and has continued to feed this cycle of victimization. The baby boomers are in their seventies and beginning to retire now. But they have created a weak generation, and thus we are on the threshold of hard times. The cycle continues on.

Another striking theory poses a similar kind of cycle. Throughout history, nations have gone through a cycle of peace and war, peace and war. If you look at a generation that's in the war, they witness firsthand the devastation and horrors of war. There is nothing romantic about it.

Those people go back home, take on political offices, and they don't want to go to war again. They know what it's like, so they strive for peace. Generation two, their children, watched dad come home broken and traumatized. They heard the horror stories of war. So, they too promote peace.

But then generation three, the grandchildren, came along and didn't grow up with the sense of war. They didn't have a close connection and or see grandpa's PTSD. This generation thinks these policies of peace are silly and unnecessary. Without that terror of war, they begin to lead the country down dangerous paths and soon enough back to war again[1].

---

1 The Strauss–Howe generational theory, also known as the Fourth Turning theory, was developed by William Strauss and Neil Howe and outlined in their 1997 book "The Fourth Turning: An American Prophecy."

The theory proposes a recurring generational cycle in American history, consisting of four turnings that repeat every 80-100 years: High (First Turning); Awakening (Second Turning); Unraveling (Third Turning); Crisis (Fourth Turning). According to this theory, each turning lasts about 20-25 years, and the cycle is driven by generational archetypes that react to the previous generation's excesses. The generation that experiences a major crisis or war (Fourth Turning) emerges with a desire for stability and peace. Their children, raised in the aftermath, continue to value peace and institutions. Grandchildren begin to question the established order. Great-grandchildren come of age during a time of crisis, potentially leading to another major conflict.

I think we're at a time where our country has experienced a long time of peace. We've had war in the Middle East and various countries, of course, but we have not had an all-out war like Vietnam or WWII. The general population has had a generous gap between such horrific violence. We don't have a cultural memory of the horrors of war. We do things that will jeopardize our peace and throw ourselves back in war, beginning right here in our own society.

Such paradigms only go to show we are in a wimpy era. Not that we need war or a Great Depression to make us strong, but we must pass on the virtues that come with perseverance through sorrow. We must uphold human dignity in order to break these cycles.

In short, we are a spoiled generation, one that has been spared the atrocities of war and have drowned in a tsunami of abundance.

Dear parents, the culture will not make your child tough; it will make your child weak. Making them tough is up to you. And this is not done by making your kid pump iron in the garage, but by making them clean the broken bottle in the garage. This is done by creating an environment of accountability, self-reliance, and grit.

A SPOILED MINDSET

The dawn of extraordinary technology has only further propelled our spoiled and corrupted dispositions. We no longer suffer in the same ways as previous generations, which is a blessing, but we suffer differently. We have severe poverty, but it is a different type of poverty.

Now, spoiled can take on many meanings. While a great many of us have been materially spoiled, I think it is more of an entitled mindset. Whether or not we have luxury cars or iPhones, our society tells us that we *must* have it, that we *deserve* it. This is our spoiled nature; this leads us into becoming self-made victims, demanding that we deserve.

As I mentioned earlier, if you're a spoiled brat in a mansion, it's somewhat easy to see that your life crumbles when somebody doesn't make the shrimp cocktail the way you like it. Of course, it's silly and absurd, but you can see that kid melting down and say, well, no wonder. We can stand back with smug hauteur at such a scene, but the reality is we would all act totally spoiled if we were all totally spoiled. We wouldn't know otherwise. And this is the case now. Culturally, we're spoiled in unprecedented ways.

Not only are we following the typical cycle and entitled mindset, but we really do have a material abundance that the world has never seen. Mass production of food, clothing, shelter, and technology, everything, and quite literally everything, is at our fingertips, just a click away.

THE DAYS OF OUR LIVES

So, how and where does this self-victimization begin? I would argue it is generally within our control. We cast ourselves into the role of a victim. Perhaps society at large initiated it, but we perpetuate it.

Think of a teenage girl who has sat and watched endless amounts of dramas on T.V. Every good story has a certain story arc to it. There's the situation and drama, there's a villain and the hero. The hero somehow becomes a victim and must overcome some feat in order to restore things back to how they should be, often much better than before. We've all seen this story. There are only a few basic storylines that are repeated time and again, after all.

Romeo and Juliet has been retold a million times. *The Lord of the Rings*, *Star Wars*, and *The Matrix Trilogy* all have basically the same premise of "the chosen one." A drama builds on itself with situation after dire situation until the tension is almost unbearable.

In this example, this teenage girl has seen all of these dramas countless times in every T.V. show and movie she's ever watched. Her whole cultural worldview is based on this drama. And every good drama has to have some kind of sacrificial victim, has to have some kind of bully. It's hard to be redeemed if you're not a victim, after all. And because society has done away with a sense of the true victim, which was us as a result of Original Sin and our need of a true redeemer, Jesus Christ, this teenager is left searching for that dynamic to be present in her life.

Such people place themselves in the movie. They place themselves in the T.V. show and they cast themselves as the victim. They want to be in the reality show or the soap opera, they want to be the hero with the horse or the beautiful couple getting married. This becomes almost a coping mechanism.

They do have legitimate problems. They have broken families, live in a crazed, manic society, and are bombarded with the world 24/7.

The social environment that they're being raised in, along with the technological environment, the religious environment, the recreational environment, the educational environment, and the professional environments, those six environments (we'll talk about these in more depth in later chapters) are really harsh environments for most people. They have not been built to foster a sense of peace and security, but rather isolation and anxiety. So, becoming a victim is a natural consequence.

This isn't entirely their own fault either. There's certainly legitimacy to this. But there is also a clear manipulation at play. This victimization is a manipulation of others, veiling truth and telling them they have nowhere else to turn. It turns attention entirely to self and self-interest.

> "True heroism is remarkably sober, very undramatic.
> It is not the urge to surpass all others at whatever cost,
> but the urge to serve others at whatever cost."
>
> *–Arthur Ashe*

Much like the Greek myth of Narcissus, the beautiful young man who falls so deeply in love with his own reflection in the water that he falls in and dies, we too have become obsessed with our own reflections.

With social media, with the way our school systems and sports teams work, the world has become a mirror. Everywhere you look, every environment that you're going into, it requires people, particularly young people, to be extremely self-conscious of how they look, what are they wearing, how they're performing, what they are saying, what group are they in. Of course, these sorts of social hierarchies have been present in society throughout history to some extent. Even the ancient Romans had hierarchies of greater togas and lesser togas (the cool kids wore nicer togas, of course).

We've now reached an all-time high where the styles and fads change so rapidly, and there are abundant resources to buy and adopt new fads so

Narcissus. Circa 1600, Caravaggio.

quickly that just to keep up with it is almost impossible. We're endlessly looking at ourselves, weighing, measuring, analyzing, just to make sure we're up to date and not left behind. It's constant. And there's so much abundance that it is impossible to keep up. We have so much "stuff" we think is so important. And when we don't have it, all we can do is obsess over getting it.

We've become spoiled to the point of believing our happiness and peace lies in getting what we want, and not what we need. We're spoiled to the point where we're bubbling over with pride and self-interest. It's purely a spoiled culture and its yolk is too much to bear.

YOUR BURDEN OF ABUNDANCE

The biggest problem with this self-victimization is that parents are adopting this troublesome notion at alarming rates.

Parents, especially younger parents, have grown up in this spoiled culture. They've grown up with total abundance (again, not only material, but in self-serving entitlement too) and it has become a great burden. Tremendous abundance is a very difficult thing to bear.

Imagine two hikers set out through the forest on a long journey. The first thinks of everything. In his pack he has a tent, plenty of high-quality food, extra pairs of clothing, pans, dishes, a little fan in case it's hot, lawn chair in case he wants to rest. He has everything with him on this long and treacherous journey, but it weighs him down. He grows more and more tired, having to stop and rest. His legs are ready to give out not even halfway through the journey. He has never been taught how to pack lean. He thinks that all of this garbage that he's carrying is necessary to survive. While at the same time, the second guy on the other trail has brought only the bare essentials. He has a small backpack and only brought what he truly needed, and he's getting through the journey so much better.

You can look at these two people and feel sorry for the idiot who is burdened because everyone told him, "Don't forget to bring your extra neck pillow." He's helplessly burdened by abundance.

Parents today feel helpless in similar ways. They feel they are victims, and you can see that parents have adopted this psychosis of self-victimization. They have a middle schooler and a high schooler, and they are so completely and totally overwhelmed.

Why? Well, there are a number of reasons. But whether it's kids in sports, both spouses having to work two jobs just to pay all the bills, keeping up with teachers at school, keeping up with the house and cars and all the day-to-day struggles, it quickly feels like you're treading water but never making it to the shore. As they grow more exhausted by the spinning world, the constant demands on them from their kids, friends, family, people slip right back into this mindset of feeling like that can't break out. They'll never get ahead; they'll never find peace. This turns into blaming everyone but themselves, and they are playing victim once again. Why? Because it's always easier to blame someone, something else than to pull yourself up and start changing your life.

So many people feel they must be perfect and do extraordinary at everything. They must work hard to move up in work, while being a perfect spouse, perfect parent, and they must be improving themselves and upgrading their life all the time. The mindset of perfection and abundance surrounds you. It's an exhausting system that traps you and makes you feel like there's no way out.

"The most extraordinary thing in the world is an ordinary man and his ordinary wife and their ordinary children."

–G.K. Chesterton

I think this abundant, busy mindset is a major culprit for making parents feel like victims. That recreational environment takes a ton of time. I remember when we were a big-time baseball family, and we had five kids on four different baseball teams at once. I certainly felt helpless. It was constant and all-consuming. The idea of my boys not playing little league baseball was anathema. So, we had to start making some tough decisions. We decided to take one season off from little league. And we never went back. These days, we wait much longer until our kids get into organized sports. Admittedly, I have 16 kids. So my situation is a little more complex than the average family. But I wish I had considered this much earlier than I had. Even with five kids, we were spinning out of control. We needed to slow down, but I was scared to do so. I wanted to "feel" like a good dad taking my kids to the field every day. Now, I'm focused on being the architect of an incredible ecosystem that provides what my kids really need to become virtuous, competent, and tough as hell.

The key thing is that these parents feel helpless because they are allowing the culture to build their infrastructure, their ecosystem, as opposed to the parents themselves building the ecosystem.

I'm not against sports. I'm not against kids playing instruments. I'm not against kids doing ballet. I'm not against vacations or any of that stuff. But parents today must remember that if the history of humanity was a 24-hour clock, kids have been playing organized sports for 20 seconds. (I did the math.[2])

It is remarkable how parents have adopted extraordinary convenience and luxury things that we have, such as organized sports, as absolute necessities for well-being. It's something that just walked on to the stage of humanity, and we assume that it's absolutely necessary to fulfill a thriving life. Parents allow the culture to build their life. Parents allow culture to be the architect of their family and they're too weak to stand up and do something about it. This is a major problem.

"You live in a deranged age, more deranged than usual because, in spite of great scientific and technological advances, man hasn't the faintest idea of who he is or what he is doing."

–*Walker Percy*

When someone else is the architect and forces you to go this way and that, and you have to do this and you have to do that, you have to buy these clothes, you have to drive this car, your kids have to do these activities, you have to live according to the standard—of course you will feel like a victim.

---

2 300,000 years of human history = 24 hours

- 1 hour = 12,500 years
- 1 minute = 208.33 years
- 1 second = 3.47 years

Now, let's calculate how many seconds 70 years represents:
70 years ÷ 3.47 years/second = 20.17 seconds

Therefore, if the entire 300,000-year history of humanity were compressed into a 24-hour clock, the last 70 years would represent approximately 20 seconds.

The Tower of Babel. Scorel, Jan van (1495-1562). Cameraphoto Arte Venezia / Bridgeman Images

In a sense, you are a victim, but you allowed yourself to become one, and you allow it to continue. And remember, this sense of self-victimization is a choice. It's a mindset we've adopted. It can absolutely change, but that requires change from you.

So, do you have the guts to say no, mom and dad? Can you say, "I'm not going to let this culture dictate how my family is built. I'm going to build it myself."

YOUR FALSE FEAR OF FAILURE

Parents also feel like victims because they feel like there's nothing they can do about it. And the reality is that this is a devastatingly shortsighted sense of their own creative powers to build a family that they choose to have.

For some reason, when people build a business, they're much more creative. They often get excited and courageous, saying, "No, this is my business. I'm going to do it the way I want to do it."

They don't let the outside world dictate to them their entrepreneurial efforts. People are far more independent and autonomous and creative and imaginative and resilient against external pressures when it comes to entrepreneurship or creativity.

But when it comes to family, we just tuck our tails, fall in line, and do what we're told.

Why is this? We have a longing to be our own person. We have a longing to be creative and imaginative and innovative and strategic and to be different than our competitors. We have a family because we longed for one and were blessed with one. Yet every day, many of us do nothing to better our families.

Many people have an extreme sense of ownership over something they've made and don't want anyone else to mess it up. They're not afraid of their business or creative work standing up and walking away saying, "I don't like what you did with me." It's theirs. It came out of their creativity.

But kids do this every day. They stand up at some point in their life and say, "I'm done with you, dad and mom. I don't want you to be my dad anymore. I don't like what you've done." Spouses do this with each other, and it's terrifying.

"Nothing is so strong as gentleness;
nothing so gentle as real strength."

–St. Francis de Sales

We've become conditioned to the falsehood that love and family and marriage are conditional. We cower when real conflict arises because we don't want to "lose" our kids or spouse. Or, on the other hand, we become overly aggressive and walk away ourselves, thinking we deserve better. But we don't work on fixing things when they're broken. We hide or walk away and allow something or someone else to take the lead.

How many parents have I met in my life that cannot bring themselves to discipline their children, particularly dads, because they are scared to death that their kid is going say, "Screw you. I'm out." Especially when they're teenagers. They are scared to death that their teenage daughter is just going to get in her car and drive away.

This goes right back into playing victim. They say, "I'm helpless here. I can't even discipline my kid because everything's against me: my spouse, my kids, my job, culture...EVERYTHING!"

I see so many dads who are scared of their own children. And they love their children. They don't want their kids to leave. So, they compromise, and compromise and compromise and compromise. Thinking that that's going to keep them close, when in reality, it doesn't.

Instead, dad and mom must demand respect but also give affection.

I think we fall into a dichotomy of thinking we can only do one or the other. But you have to give both. You have every right to. God the Father wrote it in the Ten Commandments. Honor your father and mother.

You are owed respect from your children. And they are owed affection from you.

We get into this mode of playing victim because, on some level, we're afraid of failure. We're afraid to stand up and take the reins of our family because what if we screw up? What if something happens and everyone leaves? So, we just let others take the reins and we whine and complain and remain helpless.

But you must recognize this is a false sense of failure. You must see that the culture that you have grown up in has created a self-victimization psychosis, one that is stronger than ever before in human history. If you don't recognize it, you can't fight it.

Once you do recognize it, then you're able to say, "Ok, I'm not a victim. I'm the architect."

YOU SHOULD

BE BUILDING,

NOT BUSY

C H A P T E R

2

YOU'RE NEVER TOO BUSY

One of the main reasons we feel like we're victims is because we have adopted a victim mindset. Even if we don't say out loud, "I'm a victim," we've taken on the symptoms of victimization.

As I mentioned earlier, many modern-day parents feel that they're victims because they feel so busy. But one of the things that I've diagnosed is that busy has become a bragging right. People are proud of it in a strange way. When you're super busy, you feel important. When your kids are super busy, you feel they're important. They're doing all the "right" things.

When you take a moment and research the definition of the word busy, however, it's a rather unattractive concept. People should become unattracted and unimpressed by the notion of being busy.

The First Definition

In Merriam Webster, the first definition of busy is *engaged in action; occupied.* When you hear that you think of a bathroom that just says "occupied."

Modern life has become occupied, but I hope your life is more than a porta-john that just says "occupied" or "vacant."

People often say to me, "You must be so busy," referring to how many kids I have and the amount of businesses I run. And one day as a joke it kind of flew off my tongue and I said, "Oh, I'm not busy at all. Why, are you?" They didn't even laugh. They just looked at me almost startled, and said, "What? I guess I am busy, but how are you not busy?" I told them, "No, I'm kidding. I'm busy as hell."

But I realized when I had said that, even as a joke, what it had done was elevate me to a different level of consciousness. In a sense I was saying, "I'm not busy. You're busy. Why are you busy?" Suddenly, if I have all these things I have to do but I don't consider myself busy, I have just transcended the experience of modern man. After that moment, I said to myself, "Wow. I don't want to be busy."

Every time I walk through an airport, there are people who are proud of themselves because they're members of the Admiral's Club. They paid a little extra money to have valet park their car, they get access to a fancy lounge and have a first-class seat. It seems pretty luxurious compared to the average guy who has to park in the long-term lot, take a bus to gate, and sit with all the other normal people to wait for a coach seat.

The reality is though that no matter how busy and successful those first-class people seem, the normal people and the first-classers have something in common: neither of them are successful enough to own a private jet.

If they were really so successful and had something to brag about, they'd have their own plane. They wouldn't even need to be in the Admiral's Club. They would never buy a first-class seat; they'd buy a first-class plane.

When you're busy, it's like participating in the whole airport experience, waiting in lines, going through security, waiting to take-off. But what if you never have to be busy like that again? What if you really were able to just instantly have your own plane? You never have to sit through security, never have to take your shoes off, never have to sit in the food court.

Now, you're probably not going to have your own private plane. But emotionally, psychologically, spiritually, you don't have to feel busy like everyone else does. You can free yourself from those constraints.

The Second Definition

This takes us to the second definition of busy which is: *bustling, full of activity*. When you think of bustling, you think of a little kid bouncing around, not a focused, mature, competent, dedicated individual.

People are going through their day, whether at an airport or sitting in traffic or taking the kids to practice or going to work, feeling busy, stressed, and overwhelmed. But you don't actually have to feel that way.

> "There is more to life than increasing its speed."
>
> –*Mahatma Gandhi*

It's like the man who's a bricklayer and someone asks, "What are you doing?" He says, "I'm laying bricks." Then he asks the guy right next to him and he says, "I'm building a cathedral." They're both doing the same thing, same job, but they have completely different experiences and purposes.

Busy is very much a state of mind.

When we think of the word busy, we think of being overwhelmed, stressed, can't think clearly, having so much to do. We must toil the earth, we must work and do things, but I would argue we're not supposed to be busy. We're supposed to do a lot of things. We're supposed to get a lot done. We're supposed to have a long to do list. But we don't have to be busy as we do them.

This notion of busy implies something that we don't want. Do we want to be occupied where people can't enter into our life? If you're a mom and dad, do you want to be so occupied that you can't have friends, that you can't go on a date? Do you want to be so occupied that people can't reach out and get a hold of you? No, I don't think we want that.

We're supposed to accomplish things, but are we supposed to be completely occupied so that no one can get in? No. When you think of saints, they were available and open. What kind of boss do you want? One that's so occupied you can't get a hold of them or one whose door is open.

I don't think we want a sign hanging off us that tells everybody, "I'm so important that I don't have time for you." You don't want your life to be that closed door that says occupied. You want it to say vacant. You want people to come right in.

Imagine there's a gymnast training to be in the Olympics. His whole life is committed to that one thing. And you say, "Hey, why don't you join our flag football team?"

He could respond, "I can't. I'm so busy with all of my obligations. I have a ton to do. I'm sorry. I'd love to. I just can't fit you in." Or he could say, "No. The only physical thing I do is training for the Olympics because that's my sole goal. Everything else is kind of a distraction from that. So, I'm sorry, but no."

The guy said no in both cases, but one sounds like a mess, and the other sounds like a resilient and focused individual who is on a mission. Yes, he has a lot to do, but it's not things out of his control or that he hates and is stuck doing. He is focused and trying to accomplish something. That's respectable, you get it. The Olympian is not going to play flag football.

The Third Definition

The next definition is *foolishly intrusive or meddling*. You're busying yourself in others' affairs, in other words. Meddling is to interest oneself in what is not one's concern or interfering without right of propriety. Do you want to be thought of as a meddling person? I don't think so. But here's the thing, much like being a self-made victim, many of us aren't going to self-identify as a meddler or busybody. However, when we read an article or look at the social media of some celebrity and are wondering about the divorce of two famous movie stars or wondering about some politician's affair, that's meddling.

That journalist or that social media influencer just put a whole bunch of private stuff about individuals out there for the world to see. We jump at such gossip and roll around it like pigs in mud. Our culture is crazy about meddling.

Men typically suffer from the sins of anger, lust, and sloth. And I think women suffer from the sins of pride and gossip. One thing that drives me bonkers is women will often say, "Well, I don't want to speak out of turn, and I'm certainly not trying to gossip, but I think maybe you should know this about this person so you can keep them in your prayers. They're having a lot of marriage problems and they their husband is you know, might be cheating on them, and they're having financial problems. And the daughter is having these meltdowns, and you wouldn't believe what she said. But I'm just telling you so you might say some prayers for this person."

I think such people are going to be smacked down by God Almighty. Fake charity is the worst. Using piety for the purpose of sin is grotesque.

People use prayer, God, religion, faith as a veil to cover up their horrific slander and defamation of other people's names all the time. What disgusting, filthy, devious, meddlesomeness. These people are busy and are going to pay for it.

The Fourth Definition

The fourth definition of busy is *a gaudy, distracting design, filled with junk*. That's often what our lives are like. We're so busy. Why are we proud of this?

Do you want to be full of distracting details, meddlesome, bustling about, so occupied to where important things can't access you?

I think that our world of busyness has fostered this feeling of victimization. And it's a twisted pride thing because we're saying we're so important. So many demands are placed on us. We have to pay attention to so many things because we're so important.

CHANGE YOUR MINDSET

As I said in chapter one, the first thing to do to stop being a victim is to stop thinking of yourself as a victim. It's the same here. How do you stop feeling so busy? Well, actually say, "I'm not busy."

Sundays after church, when people ask me, "Oh, staying busy?" I'll usually respond, "When I'm doing what God wants me to do, no, I'm not busy at all. But when I do what I want to do, I'm busy as hell."

That's flipping upside down the notion of busy. People pretend that busy is good. And I just flipped it upside down and say, no. Busy is bad.

"It's not enough to be busy,
so are the ants. The question is,
what are we busy about?"

–Henry David Thoreau

It's the same thing as looking at them and saying, "Don't you understand you can build your life the way you want to?" They'll look at you cross-eyed because they don't understand it.

Do you understand that you don't have to do all the things on your calendar over the next thirty days? So many people are on the verge of a panic attack because they're so busy. But if you broke your femur and had to go into the hospital and have surgery and were stuck there for a week, everything on your calendar would get canceled. It's just gone. But you don't even have to break your femur in order to do that. You can just do it.

Oh, but my kid has to do this. My kid has to do that. I have to go here. No, you don't. No, they don't.

You're choosing to do it, so take ownership of this. You have committed to activity every stinking day for the next thirty days. You did this. Not the little league soccer coach, not the dance instructor, not the teachers at the school, not your kids' friends.

You did it.

You made these choices, and you have to take ownership of your time and attention, which is the very first step in beginning to build your own environment.

Stop saying you're busy. You're never too busy. The reality is you are never too busy to do the will of God. God can give you a hundred things to do today. But if you have a hundred and fifty things on your list, fifty of them were put there by you. So, take them off. If God doesn't want you to do it, don't do it. You just got things off your to-do list. Great!

If God gives you a hundred things to do today and you're certain after prayer that He really wants you to do these hundred things, and there's only time to do eighty of them, then God wants you to fail. That's the thing we don't really recognize. We have this prosperity mindset and think that if God calls us to do all these things, He wants us to do all of them really, really well. But, as G.K. Chesterton said, anything worth doing is worth doing badly.

So, if God calls you to have a bunch of kids and have a bunch of jobs and do a bunch of things, and you're convinced that He wants you to do all of these things, don't be surprised if you fail at some of them or are mediocre at all of them. That very well may be God's desire for you. There's nothing in Scripture or Church teaching that says, if God has called you to do these things, you're going to be good at all of them.

Prosperity Gospel is full of crap.

The humbling aspect of it is that you're not called to be perfect in this worldly sense. You have to toughen up. You can't be pansies. You can't be wimps. Parenting is not for wimps. We must understand that most of these things really are within our control. You're not too busy. You must take ownership and start building your environments.

You must be the architect.

YOU ARE THE ARCHITECT.

DON'T SURRENDER

YOUR LIFE

TO THE WORLD.

CHAPTER

3

BE THE ARCHITECT

Let's talk about the etymology of the word architect.

In Greek, the word *arkhi* means "chief" and the word *tekton* means "builder" or "craftsman." This formed the ancient Greek word *arkhitekton*, meaning "master builder, director of works." A great deal of words stems from both such as Archbishop, technology, and technician.

Imagine in ancient Greece there would be many builders and technicians, but only one master builder or architect. And this is significant.

When you're on a building project, the chief builder or architect is really the one who must take ultimate ownership for so many elements of the building project, compared to an outsourcer or a contractor who's just hired to paint or lay bricks. The architect is starting with the raw material. They're looking at a vacant building site and must see what it will become.

Perhaps they have to cut down trees. They have to determine whether the ground is level, how much of it has to be brought up or brought down. They have to consider climate and the surrounding landscape. Architects in New

York City are going to be thinking about it differently than architects in the Sahara Desert versus the California oceanfront or on the side of a mountain.

The architect has to consider the natural environment. They must also consider the available resources. Do they have access to this kind of wood or this kind of stone, this kind of brick, this kind of metal? And if not, they must design something different. A good architect doesn't blame the type of wood available or the tools they have or the climate they are in. No, they must build something beautiful in spite of it all.

"You have power over your mind—
not outside events. Realize this,
and you will find strength."

–Marcus Aurelius

I'm amazed at how expensive architectural drawings are for a building. I sat on a committee when the architectural drawings alone for a particular building were one million dollars. Just the drawings. Why? Because they consider everything from the wiring to the stone to the gutters. The architectural drawings have multiple layers to it. When you have the right drawings, this gives twenty different contractors the blueprints of everything that they need. It's extremely detailed and must consider absolutely everything. It's planning out every little step. It's not just drawing a picture of what this building would look like.

So, after it's all said and done, the architect doesn't get to blame these outside sources or the contractors. They don't get to blame the environment. They have to work with the environment. Much like the old adage, "a good carpenter never blames his tools," an architect certainly can't do that either.

The famous American architect Frank Lloyd Wright famously said, "A doctor can bury his mistakes, but an architect can only advise his clients to plant vines."

There's no excuse for the architect. They have to design based on the situation. They must make the best out of what they have.

I wonder how many world class architects have used their skills to make a blueprint for family life?

STORY OF A FAUCET

Kholer, the manufacturer of kitchen and bath products, made one of my favorite commercials of all time.

Shot in elegant black and white, it depicts a renown European architect who is giving a couple a tour of his building. As they ascend uniquely crafted stairs, the architect points out photographs of beautiful, stunning buildings he's designed all over the world and all of the awards he's won. From Milan to Tokyo, he tells this couple of his unparalleled achievements in some of the world's most unique environments and landscapes. They arrive in the architect's modern, fancy office, and sit around his desk. Finally, after his stunning resume, he asks the couple, "So, what can I do for you?"

The couple glance at each other, and then the woman pulls a brushed chrome faucet from her bag and sets in on the desk in front of the architect. She says, "Design a house around this."

The architect looks at the faucet, then at the couple. Here, the Kholer name and tagline appear.

That's it. Thirty seconds long, a few lines of dialogue, and yet there's something powerful at play.

Now, why do I love that so much? Well, the creativity is incredible. They took something that was totally boring—a faucet—and they show that their brand is worthy of the greatest architect to build around it. Not a rocky mountainside or sandy beach front, but a faucet.

The commercial says that this is such a beautiful faucet that is worthy of having an architect build a house around it, as opposed to just tossing this faucet in someone else's design.

YOUR ENVIRONMENT

Imagine God gives you the most valuable faucet in the world, made of precious gems that have a trillion dollar value. So, you build a house around it. Then, you build a glorious garden around the house, and then a neighborhood full of houses around you. You then allow your closest friends and family to move in this neighborhood. Then you build a church just across that all your friends can attend. Then you put your office right next door and invite only the best people to work with you. And on and on and on. You have built an entire community around this little faucet. Why? Because it is priceless.

Your children are that faucet. What will you build around them?

You are the architect. God is saying to you, not unlike like the lady in the in the commercial, "Design a house around this." You are the master builder. It's a powerful idea.

My wife Ashley and I recently had our sixteenth child, little Monica Agnes. Now, does she come and just fit into our existing design? Or is there a little renovation that I have to start? After all, she is a unique individual. I can't assume the ecosystem I have built is exactly what she needs.

One of the other things that architects do is renovate old buildings. There are times when they're not designing from scratch. They must work with the bones of the old building but they're able to modernize it somehow while retaining a traditional look.

Every time you have a child or a major life event occurs, your job as the architect is that sort of renovation. I need to build my family a little differently today than I did two months ago before the new baby was here. And maybe you think, well, that's not really true.

To prove this point, I have imagined that she was born with extreme disability. If she needed constant care, our life would have to be reconstituted. My work schedule would have to change. The kids' educational routine might have to be amended. Our financial goals would alter radically. Our social and recreational activities, our health and fitness routines—everything would need to be reconsidered.

God bless those parents who have to do this. I am in awe at their strength and ingenuity in renovating their entire ecosystem. But therein lies my point: parents do this naturally when tragedy strikes. You and I must do it (to a far lesser extent) even when tragedy doesn't strike. With my sixteenth child, I must not assume we provide her with everything she needs. We must be open to the idea and willing to make whatever changes are necessary for her.

While it might be easy to imagine needing changes for something as drastic as that, I must still be open and look at what areas of my life might need renovation. She may not need 24/7 medical care, but she has a soul that has an eternal destination and that alone warrants renovating my family in some way, shape, or form. Being an architect is not a one-time thing. Anytime a major event happens in your life, you have to be the architect and rebuild it a little, renovate it. It's a dynamic process that is ever changing.

My wife and I went to Rome last year and stayed in this nice, old hotel. Every building in Rome is older than every building in America. We were staying in an ancient building, but it had all the modern conveniences.

A family is the same way. You get married, you have a kid, you're already developing your traditions. You have another kid, another kid, a new job, more schooling. Each time there has to be some renovation. But you're trying to retain certain sides of the tradition.

You must see your kids and spouse as that little faucet the lady sets on the table. You must build your house, your life around them because they are the most beautiful things in your life. They are worthy of having a life designed and built around them.

Being an architect is part and parcel to being a visionary. You can't really talk about being the architect of your family without talking about being the visionary as well.

While the visionary is more ethereal and contemplative, the architect is tactile and concrete. You must see yourself as both for your family. You must look and survey the land where you'll build, but you need that vision in order to make blueprints. Otherwise, you just become a builder or, worse yet, you let someone else make the designs. Being an architect is about building concrete systems in your life to realize your family's vision.

BECOMING THE ARCHITECT

How exactly does someone take on an identity or become something new?

When does someone who runs become a runner or someone who builds things out of wood become a carpenter? If you go out and run once in your life, are you a runner? Is everybody who writes an email a writer? This is a difficult thing to clearly nail down. It's hard to pinpoint when that change

Wanderer above the Sea of Fog. Circa 1818, Caspar David Friedrich

occurs, and one transforms into something new. But I believe it has something to do with frequency and intentionality.

If you run once a year, are you a runner? Probably not. If you run once a week? Probably.

I never considered myself a writer. Even after I wrote my first book, I felt like I was just a guy who wrote *If Aristotle's Kid Had an iPod.* I didn't think of myself as a writer, I didn't identify as a writer. I wrote another book, and then another. Still, I saw myself as a busy guy who wrote a few books. But then something clicked, and I thought, "Am I a writer now? When did I become a writer?"

> "We become builders by building.
> We are what we repeatedly do.
> Excellence, then, is not an act, but a habit."
>
> *–Aristotle*

It was when I found myself organizing and orchestrating my life around writing, when I was being the architect and intentionally put in time to write, that's when the change happened. Frequency met intentionality.

When you start building around the idea and buying into the fact that you're the architect of your life, you begin to shed an old identity in order to take on that new one. I would argue this process is absolutely vital. For this example, you have to shed the victim identity in order to become the architect.

Putting that mindset in place and making the declaration is important to the process. You must stand up and say it, "I am the architect of my family."

Suddenly, you will plan your schedule differently. You make time to do what you need. You become intentional and with that comes frequency. You need to begin identifying as the architect of your family and that means frequency. You need to be thinking, "I have to build this."

That means having the intentionality of, "I am the architect, not somebody else." And there's a little healthy dosage of hostility here. There must be.

> "Lead me, follow me,
> or get out of my way."
>
> *–Gen. George Patton*

If I were to go up to a couple I don't know and say, "Let me tell you how to structure your family," the husband and wife should be offended. They should want to say, "Wait just a damn minute. This is my family."

This is why when I'm on a podcast or interview and they ask me, "Well, how do you build systems? Tell us how to handle social media for our kids." I say, no. That's not my job.

My job is to empower you to make the decisions for yourself. The architect of the family builds the social media policies. The policies that I have for my seventeen-year-old are particular to my home. I can't tell you what the screen time and the social media rules should be for your family. I won't. What I am telling you is that, as the architect of your home, you must build these systems. You have to build your own systems with intentionality because there's no blueprint that'll encompass everything.

I do think, however, that there are questions that apply to everyone. There are questions that every architect must ask, including: What's the foundation like here? What's the climate like here? What materials are available to me?

The architect must ask all of the questions and then draw the blueprints.

Perhaps you say we want a sunroom. Well, do you want glass or screens? Do you want the door to open this way? What type of flooring will it have?

Much like your family's digital policy: What are the kids allowed to use? When are they allowed to use it? With whom are they allowed to communicate? What is the function, purpose, and end result?

Ask the questions, and then build.

This is where you as parents must identify as the architect. Facebook is not the architect. Instagram is not the architect. CNN and FOX News are not the architects. The little league coach, the band director, the schoolteacher, the youth minister—none of them are the architect. You are. And I want you to get a little edge in your mind, heart, and voice when you say, "Damn it, I'm the architect of my family, not you!" And when that feeling boils up a little bit inside, you know that you have finally taken ownership of your family's ecosystem and become THE ARCHITECT.

SYSTEMS AND THE ARCHITECT

You have a system for everything whether you realize it or not. You might say to yourself, well, *I don't have a system for social media.* No, actually you do. The system is leave your kids open to the throes of the Internet. *I don't have a financial system. I don't have a budget.* Well, yes, you do. Your budgetary system is spend money and see what happens.

You have systems for everything. The way you eat, the way you sleep, the way you drink, the way you walk around. Everything is a system. It's just a matter of how good or intentional that system is.

Likewise, everything has an architect. Everything.

So, the question is this: If you are not the architect for your family, who is?

If you are not going to build the systems and processes for your family, who will? I'm telling you, somebody is going to—whether it's social media, the school system, the kids next door—all the external forces will be coming in at you.

"You can't escape the responsibility of tomorrow by evading it today."

–Abraham Lincoln

Being an architect at times requires taking extreme action. Imagine that your child is in an accident and is suddenly severely handicapped. Your world changes. You have to build a new way of life, new ramps, new cabinets that the wheelchair can fit underneath, drawers, bathroom railings, all of it. You're going to plead with your boss to change your work schedule so that you can be at home more. Everything changes. And when something like that happens, you must become that architect.

It's easy to see the idea of the architect when you are literally rebuilding things in your home. But it's not easy to see yourself as the architect when everything is normal, when everything is just regularly scheduled programming, so to speak.

But that's because we can't see souls. We see handicapped legs or crying eyes, but we don't see wounded souls very well. If we saw the handicap that's present within our children's souls, however, if we saw the spiritual disabilities that are overtaking them, we would start building things faster and better than we would build ramps if our kids lost the use of their legs.

An old guy told me years ago that his wife had just had a stroke. I said, "Oh, I'm so sorry to hear that." He was an older man, upper seventies probably. And he said, "You know, I now have the most peace I've ever had." And I asked, "Really? Why?" He told me, "Because I spent my whole life trying to figure out what I'm doing with my job and every day I woke up asking, what am I going to do? And now, because my wife absolutely needs a hundred percent of my time and attention and care just to survive, I don't have to figure out anything anymore. I'm able to be at complete peace. I know day in and day out, I have to just serve her a hundred percent. There's nothing else for me to figure out because the meaningless stuff dissolves and what's important remains. For the first time in my life, I know exactly what I'm supposed to do, and I have complete peace with that."

PEACE FOLLOWS THE BLUEPRINT

There's a saying that goes, "If you're still searching, you're not committed."

Now there's some hyperbole here, but the point is that once you finish those architectural drawings, you start building, you start doing things. You're no longer trying to figure everything out. Noah might have struggled to accept God's directive to build an ark. That's easy for me to imagine. But once he told his family his plan, once he sold all he had buy the lumber, once he picked up his ax for the first time, he removed all doubt from his mind and went to work. He stopped searching for the answer and started swinging his ax. I suspect Noah was exhausted after that first day of chopping down trees. But when his head hit the pillow, he was at peace. He knew exactly what he was building for his family.

Do you?

You still have to renovate now and again, but we need some level of concrete building to have a sense of peace. If we live with the whiteboard in front of us, a blank canvas all the time, that's a lot of stress. There are too many decisions to make. You have to let the meaningless things dissolve and let what's important rise.

The point of making these decisions and commitments is so that you don't have to continually make them. It can be very stressful building the digital policy or the educational policy for your kids. But once you do it, you can actually enjoy the peace of having made the decision. You don't have to discern this all day, every day. Of course, you have to make revisions to it, just like I did last Sunday at our Quarterly Family Meeting. But once the policy is on paper, a ton of stress disappears. You have to enforce, you have to amend on occasion, for sure. But you no longer have to search all day long for how and what to do with your kid's cell phone. The problem is we very rarely get to that point.

Once you can think like the architect, there's that intentionality and you start doing it, and peace follows. Once you know what you're supposed to do, then you're ready to handle the changes as they come up. There is a real serenity that comes with having a crystal-clear blueprint for your family.

THE TWO TYPES OF SYSTEMS

As the architect, you must consider two systems or landscapes where you will build: Macrosystems and Microsystems.

We will take a closer look at macrosystems in later chapters of this book, but I'd like to briefly mention what I'm asking you to build.

For your family, you have six constituent parts that need to be built. These are the six environments, the external forces coming in at your family. I use the acronym STRREP to define this. It stands for: Social, Technological, Recreational, Religious, Educational, and Professional.

These are the environments you must build for your family.

In terms of microsystems, we won't discuss these in depth here. Those are the small daily processes such as your chore chart, your digital policy, or other smaller processes of the household. These microsystems are very important to having your household and family run with peace and order, but first you must build the foundation of your macrosystems. You must begin preparing the foundations for your building site, so to speak.

Once you have these in place, the microsystems will naturally follow.

YOU ARE

IN **CONTROL** OF

YOUR ECOSYSTEM

C H A P T E R

4

SAINT BENEDICT: THE MASTER BUILDER

As you begin to adopt your new identity as the architect of your family, you might find it helpful to look toward a mentor or role model for guidance. A personal favorite is Saint Benedict, a fourth century monk who developed the first monastic communities in Italy and who is considered the father of western monasticism.

Now, you're probably asking why am I referring to Saint Benedict? Well, Saint Benedict was a true master builder of his time and a perfect example for all of us to follow.

BIOGRAPHY OF SAINT BENEDICT

Saint Benedict was born around 480 A.D., the son to a Roman nobleman of Norcia and the twin to his sister, Saint Scholastica.

In the fifth century, the young Benedict was sent to Rome to finish his education. The subject that dominated a young man's study at this time was rhetoric—the art of persuasive speaking. A successful speaker was not one who

St Benedcit of Nursia. 1926, Hermann Nigg. Godong / Bridgeman Images

had the best argument or conveyed the truth, but one who used rhythm, eloquence, and technique to convince. The goal of the student's education was to have power of voice to convince and control, overlooking truth and humility. This philosophy was reflected in the lives of the students as well. They had everything—education, wealth, youth—and they spent all of it in the pursuit of pleasure, not truth. Benedict watched in horror as vice unraveled the lives and ethics of his companions and country.

Soon after, Benedict went to live in solitude as a hermit, spending his time in prayer and contemplation. He was constantly bombarded by the Devil, but resisted all temptations, growing deeper in his love of God.

After years of prayer, word of his holiness brought nearby monks to ask for his leadership. Slowly, Benedict and his followers began establishing monasteries where the monks lived separately. He left these monasteries abruptly when the envious attacks of another hermit made it impossible to continue the spiritual leadership he had taken.

Soon after this, he founded a monastery in Monte Cassino that became the roots of the Church's monastic system. Instead of founding small separate communities, he gathered his disciples into one whole community. No one had ever set up communities like his before or directed them with a defined rule.

Benedict had the holiness and the ability to take this risky step. His beliefs and instructions on religious life were collected in what is now known as *The Rule of Saint Benedict*—this rule still directs religious life after 1,500 years.

During Saint Benedict's time, establishing such a religious community had never been done and was somewhat unthinkable. The religious hermits and Desert Fathers all lived in isolation and followed their own individual paths.

The ideas of Desert Fathers had been prominent throughout the Christian Church for the previous hundred years or so. Benedict was drawn to a life of prayer and solitude and lived in this way for years. As he saw more and more of these monks, they began communicating and asking Benedict for advice. They were all wishing for some sort of clear path or rule to follow. Benedict brought many of them together and he developed a sort of constitution, a rule that would bring them all together to live in community so that they weren't all doing random things. Instead, they would have unity.

BENEDICTINE LIFE AND LEGACY

So why would I call Saint Benedict the master architect?

Well, in a sense, he built the most sustaining, self-perpetuating organization that the world has ever seen. Monks today, 1,500 years later, still implement exactly what he said. This is quite remarkable.

As the rule of life became clear and monks came together to live in community, they learned to farm and become craftsmen so they could sustain themselves with food and money.

Benedictine Monks, from the Life of St. Benedict. Signorelli, L. (c.1441-1523) & Sodoma, G. (1477-1549). © Dario Grimaldi / Bridgeman Images

The organizational technique of these men coming together and living behind walls and taking care of one another was so successful that communities of lay people would flock to them and begin living around the monastery.

Much of the economic infrastructure of medieval society was soon centered around a monastery. The monasteries became the center of both spiritual and cultural life. The monks provided education and are largely responsible for education becoming accessible to the average person. This was because they had scriptoriums where they transcribed manuscripts and copied the Bible and other writings. Before the printing press, this made books available throughout the world. They also started schools for all the children in the town. They became this incredible source of information and stability for the entire community.

The heart and soul of the Benedictine life, however, are the rhythms and cadence of their prayer in the Liturgy of the Hours. Together, they would pray and sing all of the Psalms. This in turn gave a particular cadence and rhythm to their community, but also the greater community built around them. Monks might bicker during the day, but then they went to evening prayer and they all sang in one unified voice. That rhythm provided a structure.

"Ora et Labora" – "Pray and Work"

When they prayed, they also rang bells. The people in the surrounding town or working in the fields would hear the bells tolling and they would pause and pray the Angelus. They would participate in this rhythm of life.

On the one hand, you could say that this life and cadence of prayer became their faucet. Everything else that was built around it naturally reflected and resembled this way of life.

Because the architecture of the Benedictine way of life was so sturdy, it preserved education, farming, economics, art, and sustained local cultures. It fostered devotion and unity.

Though we now have a post-Christian world, this Rule of Life continues to be one of the strongest foundations in human history. You know you have a master architect when the building is still standing 1,500 years later. And he not only built a building, but he built a system that would continually build buildings.

WHAT IS YOUR BENEDICT OPTION?

There's a famous book by Rod Dreher called *The Benedict Option*. Dreher's book is inspired by Saint Benedict and the monastic community, and how we too need to build our own communities. We need to build our own way of life.

In one way or another, we all can pursue that Benedictine way of life. Dreher notes some key points such as withdrawal from the mainstream secular culture to some degree. It's empowering when you realize that you don't have to participate in the nonsense of society. We think we do. But you don't have to pay attention to the news. You don't have to send your kids to terrible schools. You don't have to be consumed by social media. You don't have to.

There are many options of how you can begin, but you have to be brave and step up. Saint Benedict and his monks moved out into the desert, away from all the noise of the world, and they did fine. They left the chaos of urban lifestyle (and it was just as corrupt back then) and found peace.

Another key point Dreher makes is that Benedict and his followers were intentional about building Christian communities. We have to do the same thing. We have to withdraw from culture to some extent, and we have to be intentional about forming our community at home, our community with our friends and extended family, our technology community, our social community, our sports community, our parish community. We have to focus on education and formation. Dreher even points out that we need to engage in politics on a local level. Not the crazed whorl of national media, but we should be paying attention to what's going on in our little town, perhaps more than we're paying attention to what goes on nationally.

We need to use technology and tools much more mindfully just as good monks are very intentional about how they use tools.

A good monk is not going to allow the outside world to break in through his cell phone and interrupt his prayer and work.

According to Rod Dreher, the goal of the Benedict option is not complete isolation, but rather intentionality of building stronger Christian identities and communities to withstand the attacks of the secular world.

By living intentionally, focusing on prayer and work, mindfully designing his community and environment, Saint Benedict gives us a perfect example of what it means to be a master architect.

Now, I'm not saying move your family out to the desert and build walls around them, but you need to have some of that Benedictine mindset. You must have a little courage and gusto to say, "No, we're going to go build our own systems and structures around prayer, work, education. We're going to have rich, fulfilling relationships and communities."

Like a good architect, look at what is around you, what resources you have, and build from there. If technology and excess screens are too much, cut down on it. If your kids' educational environment is suffering, look at what options are available. Consider what you wish most for them and begin to design it. Set your rule of life in place. Build the architecture around what your family needs most.

CLOSE THE DISTANCE

In this day and age, we're all so distant. We've surrounded ourselves with social media "friends" and have become somewhat obsessed with virtual reality and artificial intelligence. We're slowly losing the ability to distinguish between what is real and what is artifice. From the food we eat to the news we hear, the lines of what is real and good are being erased.

This is why becoming the architect for your family is so important. You must build and protect a real community, a real house and place where you can exist and have a real family. You must live intentionally.

In fact, the Amish today are very similar. The Amish are fully self-sufficient communities. They don't ever have to go outside their community if they don't want to. They engage with the world on their own terms.

Now, I'm the last guy in the world that would become Amish, but I really admire how they've built a community. They have practically a zero percent divorce rate, and significantly lower rates of cancer, heart disease, obesity, diabetes, and other major health problems than the national average.

Why? Well, first of all, they're self-sufficient. They eat their own food—real food that isn't highly processed and packaged. They are active in their work and have fruitful relationships with family and friends.

When you can begin to take ownership of your environments and design them with intentionality, you can begin to find real peace. But you must let the meaningless business dissolve. You must retire from playing the self-made victim role. You must step up and discover what your family's Benedict option is.

YOU CAN'T JUST

COUNT THE DAYS, YOU

MUST **MAKE** THE

DAYS COUNT

CHAPTER

5

BUILD YOUR ECOSYSTEM

"Everyone then who hears these words of mine and does them will be like a wise man who built his house upon the rock; and the rain fell, and the floods came, and the winds blew and beat upon that house, but it did not fall, because it had been founded on the rock. And everyone who hears these words of mine and does not do them will be like a foolish man who built his house upon the sand; and the rain fell, and the floods came, and the winds blew and beat against that house, and it fell; and great was the fall of it" (Matt 7:24-27).

The words of Our Lord in the Gospel of Matthew are particularly apt to becoming the architect of your family and building your life and community on a firm foundation. While God is the Divine Artist, the one and alone Creator and Unmoved Mover, He has bestowed on us the great gift of free will. So, while it is true that God is in control, He allows us to freely choose whether or not we will heed His word. He allows us to freely choose the foundation upon which we will build our lives. He allows us to be the architect.

So far we've discussed lot of theory and defined the role of the architect. But now let's talk about how you actually begin to build your own ecosystem for your family. This is the practical application of things.

BE PROUD OF YOUR BUBBLE

We used to talk about how people lived in a "bubble." People said this in a negative way, implying that people in "bubbles" were somehow cutoff and out of touch with modern society and in turn lacking social connections or denying themselves…something.

I say, good! Live in a bubble. Be proud of your bubble. These used to be known as families and communities. So, embrace it. Build your own bubble.

With the six external factors I mentioned earlier (social, technological, recreational, religious, educational, and professional) that are coming in at your family, you have to figure out how you will manage them. This requires building your own bubble, or ecosystem, as I call it. It requires vision and intentionality to craft your ecosystem, and it demands courage to not let anything destroy it.

WHAT IS YOUR ECOSYSTEM?

An ecosystem is the combination of multiple environments coming together to form a system that lives off of each component. Ecosystems, such as rainforests, have certain vegetation, animals, and climates. All these little environments converge and form one ecosystem. Each of the six external forces are individual environments. When they all come together within your family, this creates a larger, more delicate ecosystem.

Your job is to manage and balance these environments to keep things level and healthy.

"Do all you can, with what you have, where you are."

–Teddy Roosevelt

If the ecosystem of a rainforest gets too much water, let's say, certain plants and insects die. If a drought comes one year, other things will begin to wither and die off, animals might be forced to migrate, and balance gets off.

In the same way, your family's ecosystem is just as delicate and must be kept in balance.

Let's take a closer look at each of these environments.

Social Environment

Your social environment deals mostly with friendships and relationships. These might be your neighbors, kids at school, teammates, or family.

It is your job as the architect to see all of these dynamics, the people, the locations, and build the appropriate walls to protect your family, along with the appropriate bridges to connect with good outlets.

The social life of our children, spouses, and ourselves affects us substantially. This is why you need to be intentional and ask yourself: What is the social life here? How can I improve it? What does this offer to my family?

Technological Environment

The technological revolution has affected families and society in myriad ways. This includes games, streaming services, music, social media, texting, email, smartphones, etc. While these can be great tools and bring joy and entertainment, they can often be extremely overwhelming and lead to critical problems.

The architect must see technology as an environment in and of itself that you have to construct. You must manage it and build systems to handle it appropriately.

In Well-Ordered Family™, the Digital Policy Builder™ is a great tool to help with this (scan the QR code above to learn more). By establishing a digital policy for your family, you ask questions such as: What works and what doesn't? What is the purpose of this technology? When are we allowed to use it? Who is allowed? Where are they allowed? And so forth.

Now, every family already has a digital policy. Perhaps you're thinking, "No, we don't have one." But yes, you do, because that's your policy. You allow free reign and use of technology without boundaries. But if you take an honest assessment of this, does it really work? Is it the best way to manage this environment?

Creating a digital policy for your family is necessary and it must be unique to your family alone. What works for my family won't work for my neighbors or for you. You must be intentional and define how much or how little you will allow this environment to work within your family life.

Recreational Environment

The recreational environment is particularly susceptible to imbalance and causing a lot of problems. You as the architect need to be very aware of this environment.

This environment includes sports, music or dance lessons, or any extra-curricular activity you or your children do. This is similar and overlaps with your social environment, but still very different.

If your kids play football, for example, they're going to naturally have social influence from teammates and coaches. Each of these environments intersect to some degree and introduce other parts of other environments.

If your kids are on a team in high school, you better believe that technology is going to factor into that. So, you must be intentional and build the recreational environment that you want, recognizing that it interrelates with social and technological.

On one hand, recreation is good on a number of levels for interacting with other kids, learning a sport or skill, and, obviously, exercise is necessary to be healthy. Pope Pius XII said, "Sport, properly directed, develops character, makes a man courageous, a generous loser, and a gracious victor. It refines the senses, provides mental clarity, and prepares people to be gracious, humble, and hospitable." But it takes an unhealthy turn when you're driving kids to cross country, then soccer, then dance. Traveling all over the state for tournaments, pouring tons of money into this recreational activity for your seven- or eight-year-old. When you start pushing them and creating undue pressure to perform and excel in all these false ways, it can get very dangerous. Sure, you might hope or dream that they're going to be the next Tom Brady or Mia Hamm, but the reality is, no, probably not. But also, more importantly, it's not about that. It's not solely about competition. It's about something deeper, something better that your children are doing and so you have to set those boundaries.

Youth sports in this country have become particularly unbalanced and blown out of proportion. You now have five- and six-year-olds on travel baseball teams, going all over the country. Swim teams that practice seven days a week. The pressure to perform for these young kids is absurd, but it becomes an obsession for parents because of the thousands and thousands of dollars they've poured into it for some reason. But this is simply out of balance.

Aristotle said that virtue stands in the mean between extremes. This is particularly important for you as the architect to remember.

On one extreme, never allowing your kids to play sports, or not introducing them to the physical feats of the human body is a shame. It's important for us as humans to exert ourselves, body, mind, and soul, in order to achieve a certain goal. Friendly competition is good because it drives us to be as best as we can.

Socrates once said, "It is a shame for a man to grow old without seeing the beauty and strength of which his body is capable." There's a lot of truth in that.

It's good to push our bodies to some level, especially when we're young. It humbles us and it is good to use our bodies to their full extent.

On the other extreme, there is the obsession with sports. This is where the body is seen simply as a tool as opposed to it being dignified. Bodybuilders can suffer from something called "angelism" where they almost think they're angels or divine in some way. Their body is nothing more than a tool that they get to construct the way they want it to be as opposed to it being a living, breathing, dignified thing.

My point is that this environment can become very dangerous. On one extreme you have obsession, and on the other you have a slothful indifference to physical activity. The virtue of recreational activity lies in between these points. You and your children absolutely should have physical activity. Does this mean organized sports? Maybe, but it doesn't have to. It could be a family hike. It could be getting outside to fish, or swim, or ski. You should let the body flourish.

As the architect, find the virtue between the extremes.

Religious Environment

I see this as its own environment because for people that have a strong church community or spiritual life, this becomes a hub for them. It intersects with social and recreational life quite often as well. For many of us, our religious life becomes much like that Benedictine monastery where everything is kind of rotating around it.

People that have a really strong church life also find their social life there as well. A lot of their recreation likewise comes from there. Maybe your kids are participating in the youth group or church sports leagues. Many parents also send their children to Catholic or Christian schools and Sunday School.

There are many benefits to a strong church community. As the architect, you need to be very conscious about building and seeing how your religious environment is affecting the other environments.

Educational Environment

Clearly, parents need to be very intentional about the educational world that their kids are living in. What school am I sending them to? What are their teachers like? What are the kids like? What's the curriculum? There are a lot of options and questions here.

Is your public school district best for your kids? Or perhaps should you look into private education? Are there grants or scholarships you can apply for to give your kids a better educational environment? Perhaps homeschooling is what you most need.

I'm amazed how most people think, "Oh, I could just never homeschool." But really, I think they are looking at homeschooling the wrong way. There are so many wonderful curriculums and programs now that can provide excellent opportunities and balanced education for your kids.

No matter what, you have to be intentional about these factors. You have to be very proactive in managing this environment and constructing it. You shouldn't passively hand your kids over to a school system and expect them to handle everything perfectly. They have their own way of building and managing. But remember, you can't let them be the architect for your kid's education. You are the architect.

Even beyond the school systems, it is your job to foster a culture and love of learning in your home. This is very important because the home is where education and formation begin. If you have this, if education begins and is sustained at home, the environment will follow into public or private schools. Just as you might encourage your children in sports, you must push and encourage them in learning.

Professional Environment

The professional environment mostly applies to mom and dad, but it can also have a hefty impact on the family when teenagers get their first job.

How you handle your work and life balance is very important. Will you allow your work to invade and take over your family life? Do you let the stress of your boss or coworkers affect you?

Or perhaps you're helping your kids move out of the nest and enter into the big world. You have to help them figure out how to maneuver the professional world. How do you help them deal with a nasty boss or inappropriate colleagues? This can be very hard, and you can't shelter your kids from it forever.

Again, as the architect have to decide how much you will let the kids out of the nest. How much are you going let yourself or your teenager be influenced by bad people at work? This is different than social life. It's connected, but your social environment are friends; much different than your professional life and relationships. Maybe you think social life is so much more important, yet you'll spend a lot more time at work. You might spend only an hour a week with your best friend but you're going to spend eight hours a day with your boss and coworkers. Keeping your professional environment balanced is vital to your family life.

LIVE WITH INTENTION

I've used this word several times now, but I think it's important that we define it. Often people will use *intention* and *purpose* interchangeably. But they're very different.

Where purpose is the reason why you do something or the end result, doing something with intention means being aware of your purpose and aligning your actions with your virtues.

So, in all that you do, especially when building, managing, and renovating your ecosystem and community, do it with intentionality. Be aware of your purpose and align your actions with your virtues.

You should stand back and see how all of these environments intersect and react to each other. Just like gears in a clock, where one begins to move, it moves all the others with it. They're connected. You must be aware of these connections and reactions, and act upon them with intention.

The trick is to get them all turning in the right way at the right time. This is where you fine-tune your architectural skills.

THE FAMILY STRREP TEST

Another tool I introduce in the Well-Ordered Family™ system is the Family STRREP Test™. This is a wonderful tool to help you assess the most important factors of each of these six environments (STRREP stands for those six environments: social, technological,

recreational, religious, educational, and professional). I would encourage you to use this for your family.

The STRREP Test helps you to take a closer look at each of these environments and analyze how they are currently working for your family. The results might come back positive or negative, but that's all right. This gives you and your family the chance to renovate and manage these environments to better fit the life you want.

YOU CAN'T OUTSOURCE

One final point I'd like to make about building your ecosystem is that you can't outsource the design. You can outsource small tactical things, but not the design.

You have to own it. You have to live it. You have to be intentional with it.

As the architect, you will end up building seven different parts. You have your six external environments, and the seventh is the master ecosystem that connects them all. But you must build them with intention and vision, aligning purpose with virtue. If you allow someone else to design it and make the blueprints, it will follow their intention and their vision. You can't outsource the design of your family's ecosystem.

You are the architect. You are the master builder.

CONCLUSION

Dear Reader,

Though this may be a little book, it carries a big weight. But it is a good weight, a necessary weight. You were not placed on this earth to be weightless—that is, free from responsibility, free from being the best steward of your life and family. Far from it. You are called to be a saint. You are called to bring as many people to heaven with you as you possibly can. The first and foremost way you can do this is by leading your family in virtue.

Being a leader means dealing in hope. As the architect you must see the obstacles and troubles. You must name them so you can tame them. In this way, you will most assuredly bring hope in what appear to be hopeless situations.

When you can break free from the cycle of being a victim, when you change your mindset from being busy to building; when you can design and build your family's ecosystem, you will see the fruits of peace and joy from your labors.

Being a parent takes guts. Being a husband or wife takes guts. You can't sleepwalk your way through these delicate relationships, nor be passive toward the wolves who threaten your family's wellbeing. Well…you can. But trust me, it doesn't end well. Just look around. Look at the depression, the broken families, the lost souls, the addicted souls. Evil is real and it abounds. It finds any entry point and enters like a slow leak. Ignore it, and soon you're up to your neck.

This is not to say you should be afraid or anxious or despairing. Far from it! You must arise, take ownership over what God has allotted you. Whether it be a mansion or tent, one child or twelve, it's time for you to become the architect and protect what is most precious. It takes guts, it takes hope, and it takes love. But you contain all of these. You contain multitudes of virtue and grit, but you can't passively wait around for them to show up. You must practice them. You must live them.

You have been blessed with being the leader and visionary of your family. You have been blessed to be the architect of your life. So arise and begin.

IMAGE CREDITS

p. 4 Portrait of William Shakespeare (1611) / Artist: John Taylor / National Portrait Gallery, https://en.wikipedia.org/wiki/File:William_Shakespeare_by_John_Taylor,_edited.jpg / Source, Photographer: https://www.npg.org.uk/collections/search/portrait.php?search=ap&npgno=1&eDate=&lDate= / User:Dcoetzee / Licensing: Public domain, via Wikimedia Commons

p. 6 Four-step process chart © Artos, Shutterstock.com

p. 13 Narcissuss, circa 1600/ Artist: Caravaggio (1571–1610), https://en.m.wikipedia.org/wiki/File:Narcissus-Caravaggio_(1594-96)_edited.jpg / Source, Photographer: Hohum / Collection: Galleria Nazionale d'Arte Antica / Licensing: Public domain, via Wikimedia Commons

p. 15 G. K. Chesterton(1909) / Photographer: Ernest Herbert Mills, https://commons.wikimedia.org/wiki/File:Gilbert_Chesterton.jpg / Source: National Portrait Gallery: https://www.npg.org.uk/collections/search/portrait.php?search=ap&npgno=x134952&eDate=&lDate= / Licensing: Public domain, via Wikimedia Commons

p. 17 The Tower of Babel (oil on panel) / Scorel, Jan van (1495-1562) / Netherlandish / Photo credit Cameraphoto Arte Venezia / Bridgeman Images

p. 18 Saint Francis de Sales, https://commons.wikimedia.org/wiki/File:Saint_Fran%C3%A7ois_de_Sales.jpg / Source: http://www.santosebeatoscatolicos.com/2015/01/sao-francisco-de-sales-bispo-e-doutor.html / Author: Unknown / Licensing: Public domain, via Wikimedia Commons

p. 22 Socrates, ancient greek philosopher © Anastasios71, Shutterstock.com

p. 26 Henry David Thoreau (18 June 1856) / Author: B.D. Maxham, https://commons.wikimedia.org/wiki/File:Benjamin_D._Maxham_-_Henry_David_Thoreau_-_Restored_-_greyscale_-_straightened.jpg / Source: National Portrait Gallery; https://en.wikipedia.org/wiki/National_Portrait_Gallery_(United_States) / Licensing: Public domain, via Wikimedia Commons

p. 30 Bust of Marcus Aurelius (0170s) / Artist: Unknown, https://en.wikipedia.org/wiki /File:MSR-ra-61-b-1-DM.jpg / Collection: Musée Saint-Raymond / Source: Photothèque du musée Saint-Raymond / Author: Daniel Martin / Licensing: Public domain, via Wikimedia Commons, Creative Commons Attribution-Share Alike 4.0 International (CC BY-SA 4.0): https://creativecommons.org/licenses/by-sa/4.0/deed.en

p. 34 Wanderer above the Sea of Fog (circa 1818) / Artist: Caspar David Friedrich / Collection: Hamburger Kunsthalle / Source, Photographer: https://www.tiqets.com/ja/hamburg-attractions-c64886/tickets-for-hamburger-kunsthalle-skip-the-line-p976728 / Licensing: Public domain, via Wikimedia Commons

p. 35 General George Patton (1945), https://en.m.wikipedia.org/wiki/File:General_George_Patton_by_Robert_F._Cranston,_Lee_Elkins,_and_Harry_Warnecke,_1945,_color_carbro_print,_from_the_National_Portrait_Gallery_-_NPG-NPG_95_404Patton -000002.jpg / Photographer: Robert F. Cranston, Harry Warnecke, Lee Elkins / Collection: National Portrait Gallery / Source: National Portrait Gallery: https://npg.si.edu/object/npg_NPG.95.404 / Licensing: Creative Commons CC0 1.0 Universal Public Domain Dedication

p. 37 Abraham Lincoln, https://commons.wikimedia.org/wiki/File:Abraham_Lincoln_O-77_matte_collodion_print.jpg / Photographer: Alexander Gardner / Credit: Moses Parker Rice (1839-1925), possibly one of Gardner's former assistants, copyrighted this portrait in the late nineteenth century, along with other photographs by Gardner. Collection: Mead Art Museum / Source: https://museums.fivecolleges.edu/detail.php?t=objects&type=ext&f=&s=&record=0&id_number=1947.135 / Licensing: Public domain, via Wikimedia Commons

p. 42 St Benedcit of Nursia. Hermann Nigg 1926. (1849-1928). Heiligenkreuz Abbey, Vienna, Austria / Photo credit: © Godong / Bridgeman Images

p. 43 Benedictine Monks, from the Life of St. Benedict (fresco) (detail) / Signorelli, L. (c.1441-1523) & Sodoma, G. (1477-1549) / Photographer: Dario Grimaldi / Photo credit © Dario Grimaldi / Bridgeman Images

p. 44 Saint Benedict Medal © Allexxe, Shutterstock.com

p. 50 Theodore Roosevelt (1904) / Source: This image is available from the United States Library of Congress's Prints and Photographs division under the digital ID ppmsca.35645 / Author: Pach Brothers; restored by Adam Cuerden / Licensing: Public domain, via Wikimedia Commons

p. 53 Discus thrower, ancient marble statue © Andrea Izzotti, Shutterstock.com

p. 9 *(Sample Chapter)* Ritratto di Sebastiano Valfrè / https://commons.wikimedia.org/wiki /File:Ritratto_di_Sebastiano_Valfr%C3%A8,_1834-1835_-_Accademia_delle_Scienze_di _Torino_-_Ritratti_0009_B.jpg / Source-Photographer: Archivio storico dell'Accademia delle Scienze di Torino / Artist: Francesco Gonin / Collection: Academy of Sciences of Turin / Licensing: Public domain, via Wikimedia Commons

p. 14-15 *(Sample Chapter)* Chalkboard © STUDIO DREAM, Shutterstock.com

p. 17 *(Sample Chapter)* Ernest Hemingway at his typewriter, circa 1939 / https://commons.wikimedia.org/wiki/File:ErnestHemingway.jpg / Source: http://www.phoodie.info/2013/07 /19/from-the-desk-of-ernest-hemingway-this-weekend-cuba-libre-celebrates-my-birthday / Author: Lloyd Arnold / Licensing: Public domain, via Wikimedia Commons

RECOMMENDED READING

Well-Ordered Family: *The Family Management System*

by Conor Gallagher

Do you yearn for more order and clarity within your family? Is the chaos and busyness of modern life unsettling the harmony of your household? Conor Gallagher, CEO of multiple businesses and father of fifteen, unveils a transformative system in Well-Ordered Family that will restore peace and joy in your household.

In his proprietary system, Conor has applied best business practices to the challenges of family life. The Well-Ordered Family Management System™ is broken down into six parts:

- **Vision:** Establish a clear path forward for your family, crafting a vision statement and defining your long-term goals.
- **Unity:** Institute a cadence of family meetings to help the family stay aligned around a shared vision.
- **Systems:** Implement effective macro and micro systems, creating environments and routines that foster efficiency and harmony.
- **Metrics:** Track and manage vital aspects of family life with simple, non-intrusive metrics that drive positive change.
- **Relationships:** Understand and leverage individual temperaments for stronger, healthier connections.
- **Discernment:** Use decision-making and problem-solving tools to guide your family through the daily challenges of life.

Packed with more than twenty-five practical tools, including worksheets and sample processes, Well-Ordered Family is a compass for families to reclaim order and clarity. Discover how business principles can revolutionize family life.

Join Conor Gallagher on this transformative journey to create a well-ordered family—because the grace you seek starts with the order you build.

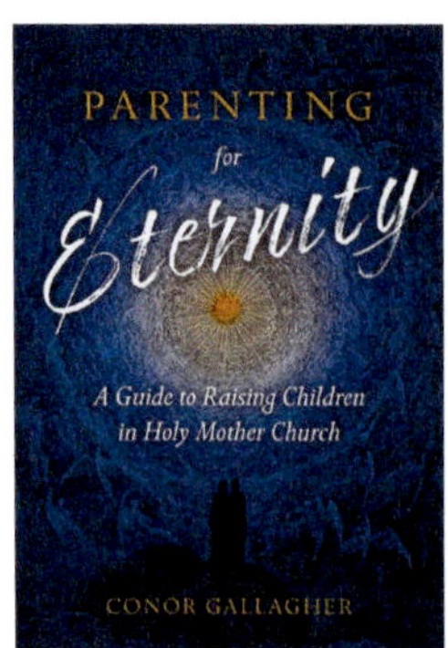

Parenting for Eternity: *A Guide to Raising Children in Holy Mother Church*

by Conor Gallagher

A trillion years from now, your child will be either in Heaven or in Hell. And this is only the beginning of eternity.

In light of this eternal perspective, the time is now, Dear Parent, to raise your child to live entirely for Christ and His Church. The time is now to train your child in the Four Last Things, the spiritual life, the virtues of piety and humility, and the school of Calvary while shielding him from the errors of modernism, Protestantism, and much more.

Unlike most parenting books which focus exclusively on the body and this fleeting world, this short work focuses upon your child's eternal soul. In these pages, you will be challenged to see the eternal consequence of every single parental act—acts of commission and acts of omission.

The Lord has said unto you, it is better that you have a millstone hung around your neck and that you be cast into the depths of the sea than for you, Dear Parent, to lead your little one astray (Mk 9:41).

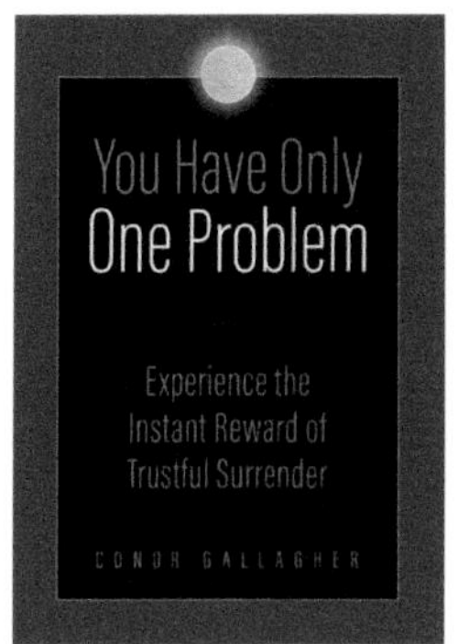

You Have Only One Problem: *Experience the Instant Reward of Trustful Surrender*

by Conor Gallagher

You have a very big problem. Not a hundred, not dozens, not ten, but one—and it's a big one. Most of us put out fires on a daily basis, whether they be dirty diapers, bills to pay, car trouble, fractured familial relationships, or the dramas of your social circle. Our self-centeredness pulls us into these struggles and blinds our perspective to the greater truth that all of these stem from one core problem.

Perhaps the greatest misconception you carry in your mind and heart is that your suffering is bad or wrong or that it is in some other way a serious "problem." This little book will challenge that idea. It will help you see that, more often than not, your suffering is not your "problem" but a perfectly designed gift from God to bring you instant happiness.

So, what is your real "one problem"?

"Your one and only one problem is this: that you have not completely surrendered yourself and every part of your life to Divine Providence."

In *You Have Only One Problem*, Conor Gallagher, father of sixteen and CEO of TAN Books, takes you through an introspection that will change the way you approach the inevitable difficulties of life. This short book is easy to get through, but it is hard to read, for it pierces the soul with a straight edge on every page. With spiritual candor and frequent references to saintly examples, this book will make you stop and think about your sufferings in a completely new way. It will enable you to accept your joys and sorrows with the same frame of mind that countless saints have had before.

Trustfully surrendering to Our Lord is the only way to have no problems in this life. You cannot surrender 80 percent of yourself or 90 percent. You have to fully and completely surrender to Divine Providence—100 percent. Only then will you see all your perceived problems as they truly are: sanctifying gifts for your salvation. You will finish this little work with a perspective that can be perfectly summed in this simplest of prayers: *Lord, I wish to only wish what you wish.*

You are Never Too Busy: *Seeing Your Time the Way God Sees Your Time*

by Conor Gallagher

What if you could never be "busy" again?

You always feel busy, with your to-do lists and packed calendars. There are kids' baseball practices, work lunches, sales presentations, home projects, and monthly bills. The list goes on and on and always will.

Upon reflection, you might admit that you take a little pride in how busy you are. This is why the question "How you doing?" is so often answered with the single word "Busy!"

But as author Conor Gallagher says, "Being busy might not be what you think it is. It really means that you are, in a manner of speaking, lost or out of control. It means the world has more power over you than God does."

As a free human, you *always* have time—plenty of time—to do God's will. The reason you might not see this clearly is the secret sin of modern times; not the sin of pride, or lust, or gluttony, but the oft-overlooked sin of sloth. How ironic it is that the busy person is often really guilty of being slothful!

In this short book, Gallagher, father of sixteen and CEO of TAN Books, will have a lasting impact on you as you hustle and bustle your way through life. His words will calm you and refocus you on your deepest desire: to do God's will.

Anyone who suffers from the anxiety of a "busy" life needs to read this book. It will show you how the saints were never busy and help you eradicate busyness from your daily life. You will finally discover peace and serenity amidst the chaos of the modern world.

"You are about to begin your journey to total freedom of time. Your time belongs to you and God. No one else. His gift to you is to never be busy again."

Still Amidst the Storm:
A Family Man's Search for Peace in an Anxious World
by Conor Gallagher

The apostles are trapped in a mighty storm, their fishing boat on the brink of capsizing . . . and Jesus slept. This confused, scared, and even angered the apostles, who could not fight back the storm. But as always, Christ is our model.

In these modern times, we often find ourselves adrift in a storm of stress, anxiety, and chronic busy-ness. We all suffer from it. In these moments, it's easy to react like the apostles: to panic, to become angry, to be frightened.

But like Christ, we should strive to be still amidst the storm. Here, Conor Gallagher (as a father of 15, no stranger to life's chaos) helps you reflect upon and cultivate three remedies to the stress of modern life:

- encountering God in the present moment, which requires a stillness of mind, to remain in the moment instead of fretting over past mistakes or future anxieties
- listening to the voice of God, which can only be heard by blocking out the relentless noise of the world and calming our increasingly restless souls
- resting in serene stillness by resisting the stir-crazy spirit of the world and rejecting busy-ness for busy-ness's sake

In a world that constantly bombards us with noise, this little book offers a wealth of practical advice and real-world guidance on how to cut out stress, anxiety, and worry so that we may rest in the Lord and hear His voice, so that we may be *Still Amidst the Storm.*

Humility of Heart

by Fr. Cajetan Mary da Bergamo

This is the greatest book on humility ever written and will likely be the best book you will read in the next 5 years (outside of Holy Scripture). If everyone in the United States would adhere to the advice in this book, we would convert the world.

Here is how the book opens up:

"In Paradise there are many Saints who never gave alms on earth: their poverty justified them. There are many Saints who never mortified their bodies by fasting or wearing hair shirts: their bodily infirmities excused them. There are many Saints too who were not virgins: their vocation was otherwise. **But in Paradise there is no Saint who was not humble.**"

Below are a few more gems of wisdom contained in *Humility of Heart.* Fr. Cajetan da Bergamo has assembled in this incomparable Catholic classic every conceivable motive for us to practice the virtue of humility.

"It is only by the measure of thy humility that thou canst hope to please God and save thyself, because it is certain that God 'will save the humble of spirit.'" (Ps. 33:19—Page 60).

"As paradise is only for the humble, therefore in paradise everyone will have more or less glory according to his degree of humility." (Page 75).

"Humility generates confidence, and God never refuses His grace to those who come to Him with humility and trust." (Page 93).

From every direction, he marshals up the reasons why this virtue is paramount in the lives of all saints and of all those on the way of perfection. As no one will enter Heaven who is not perfect and as no one will gain perfection who is not humble, it behooves us all to apprise ourselves of the requisites for gaining true humility of heart, for once possessing this virtue, we can then make great strides in the spiritual life. But without it, we are simply deceiving ourselves regarding our spiritual progress and postponing the great work of our own salvation.

"The prayer of him that humbleth himself shall pierce the clouds." —Ecclesiasticus 35:21

Trustful Surrender to Divine Providence: The Secret of Peace and Happiness

by St. Claude La Colombière,
Fr. Jean Baptiste Saint-Jure

To trust in God's will is the "secret of happiness and content," the one sure-fire way to attain serenity in this world and salvation in the next. *Trustful Surrender* simply and clearly answers questions that many Christians have regarding God's will, the existence of evil, and the practice of trustful surrender, such as:

- How can God will or allow evil?
- Why does God allow bad things to happen to innocent people?
- Why does God appear not to answer our prayers?
- What is Trustful Surrender to Divine Providence?

This enriching classic will lay to rest many doubts and fears and open the door to peace and acceptance of God's will. TAN's pocket-sized edition helps you to carry it wherever you go, to constantly remind yourself that God is guarding you. He does not send you any joy too great to bear or any trial too difficult to overcome.

AN EXCERPT FROM ANOTHER BOOK IN THIS SERIES...

A
Well-Ordered Family
Short Read

RAISING BLUE-COLLAR KIDS IN A WHITE-COLLAR WORLD

Toughening Up Your Kids with

GRIT & GRACE

CONOR GALLAGHER

GALLAGHER

RAISING BLUE-COLLAR KIDS IN A WHITE-COLLAR WORLD

TAN

CONTENTS

CHAPTER

1

DITCHING THE WHITE-COLLAR MINDSET

What is a blue-collar kid? Or better yet, what does it mean to raise a kid with a blue-collar soul? It has nothing to do with one's career or how much money one makes. It has nothing to do with status in society or one's intelligence. Someone with a blue-collar soul is in fact rather ordinary, and this, most especially in today's world, makes them extraordinary. It begins with clearing your soul of the world's dust, which falls like glitters of gold flaking off the golden calf of the white-collar world. It begins with emptying oneself of pride and sloth. In regards to our kids, it begins with helping them avoid pride and sloth. In short, it begins with humility and grit for you and me, your kids and my kids.

This, dear parents, is the blue-collar soul. And this book is my explanation of why you need to raise your kids to have a blue-collar soul in a white-collar world.

THE STORY OF A PRESIDENT

When I was a child, my dad told me a story about Ronald Reagan that I've never forgotten.

During his presidency, Reagan was often described as the most powerful man in the world. And yet, the president was shockingly humble and modest. Vice President George H.W. Bush recalled experiencing this when he went to visit him in the hospital after the 1981 attempted assassination of Reagan. The visit stuck with the vice president long after.

As he entered the hospital room, the vice president saw that Reagan wasn't lying in his bed. He looked around and almost left when the familiar voice said, "Hello, George." The vice president turned to find Reagan on his hands and knees in the bathroom. "Are you all right, Mr. President?" Bush asked. Reagan smiled and explained that he had spilled some water and was wiping it up. "I don't want the nurses to have to mop it up," he said. "I'm enough of a nuisance to them as it is. Be with you in a second." Bush later stated in an interview, "That's the sort of man Ronald Reagan was."

Now, this is a perfect example of humility and modesty, two virtues I've tried to practice every day. But more so, this is an example of a man who had a blue-collar soul and mindset. This is what we must teach our children to become.

In the simplest way, it begins with humility. In this anecdote from President Reagan's life, we see a man who had the whitest collar job possible—he wouldn't need to lift a finger to do anything if he didn't wish, and no one would blink an eye or judge him for it. And yet, there he was doing one of the most humble things ever—cleaning up a bathroom floor.

Now, this may seem inconsequential to you, it may seem like a nice thought but has no bearing on real life. But if you can't see the beauty in this story, then close the book now. Let me ask you this, dear parents: If your kid is president, will he clean up his own spill so the maid doesn't have to?

This is at the heart of the matter concerning our children and society today. We've lost something very important as we've gained and acquired so much trash. We've forgotten what it means to live humbly, to push ourselves out of comfort and into something far better. We've become afraid of real, hard work, and we've tried to spare our children such hard work as well.

We've exchanged grit for comfort. But the harsh truth is that by giving your kid everything, you're taking everything away.

THE 40% RULE

Retired U.S. Navy SEAL Dave Goggins developed what is now known as the "40% rule." This he learned during his training and career as a SEAL. Goggins' rule states that when you think you've reached your limit or think you're done, you're actually only 40% done, and you still have 60% left in the tank.

This rule is another example demonstrating the essence of a blue-collar soul: they understand hard work, they know that when they've reached a perceived limit, they still have more to go.

> "You are in danger of living a life so comfortable and soft, that you will die without ever realizing your true potential."
>
> *–David Goggins*

Your kids need to understand this. They need to understand that when they first encounter an obstacle it is usually, by nature, an easy limit to overcome. Things become hard progressively. Thus, a small amount of effort never encounters a high degree of difficulty. Tough people know this. They know that suffering is endured for a good deal of time before they overcome it. But the wimp? The first sign of difficulty cripples them. They confuse it with a true limit, an immovable object, a barrier they are unable to scale, a suffering they are unable to endure. By developing the virtue of fortitude, or perseverance, one's threshold for suffering grows and grows and grows. It's not unlike the very first time you stretch and try to reach your toes. It hurts that first time, but you know the more you try, the father you will reach. But if you quit at that first sign of pain, at the first pangs of suffering, you will never know the fruits of what lies beyond. Your job as parents is to help your kids push beyond those perceived limits.

Hear me, Christian Parent: *you* have a grave moral duty to teach your child to suffer well.

Perceived limits are at an all-time low in this society because of our age of comfort, leisure, and commercialism. Children are being pacified to such sad extremes. Especially when both parents have to work, it's often easier to give the kids what they want to make the suffering pass. We give them technology, we give them crappy food, we comply and compromise with tantrums. In one sense, the super busy parents are pacifying their children to make their own life easier. Do you realize how hard it is to make your kids do their chores? Sometimes it's easier for me to just do the darn chore than getting the kids to do it.

But remember, dear parent: Thou shalt not rob thy kids of the moral fruit of doing their chores.

STRONG PARENTS CREATE STRONG KIDS

In our complicated modern world, there's nothing wrong *per se* with two working parents. These days, it's extremely difficult to maintain a single income household. But when both parents are working what can easily happen is that your kids are forgotten and left to their own devices. They're pacified with T.V., video games, endless sports practices, etc., because mom and dad are busy. This can also happen with a mom or dad who's at home but are lazy. You can have lazy parents whether they're working or not. Parents can be home all day and still spoil their kids because they're not truly engaged with them. In essence, it becomes this dynamic of: It's just easier for me to do the dishes myself. It's just easier for me to clean the playroom. It's easier for me to cut the grass than to teach my teenager how to do it. It's easier for me to do these things because training a child in the art and science of life is a very difficult, demanding, and frustrating activity.

More likely, however, is the dynamic where you fear making your kid work hard. You fear them revolting against you. I see this all the time. Parents can't communicate tough lessons because the teenager might say, "Whatever man! I'm out!" Is your relationship with your son and daughter not strong enough to withstand a little discomfort? The irony is that strong parents who deliver strong messages create strong bonds with their kids. Weak parents who can't deliver strong messages create weak bonds.

> "Here is the self-fulling prophesy: your fear of ruining the relationship ruins the relationship."

I am teaching my kid how to drive right now and, honestly, I hate doing it. Driving myself is much easier. But if you're a parent who has a 15-year-old with a driver's permit, you have a moral duty to make them drive as much as possible before they get their license. No matter what. When I'm in a hurry and I want to get somewhere I have to take a deep breath and make him drive. When it's pouring rain and I'm nervous about him driving, I have to make him drive so that he learns. I have to make the painstaking effort, which I hate doing, and make him drive. Why? Because I have to use all of those opportunities to train him to be a good driver before he gets in the car by himself. There is a moral duty to maximize that time and train your kids. Parents that let their kids get a driver's permit and never get in the car with them, never teach them, are morally incompetent. Lives are at stake, and soon their kid is on the highway, driving through town, completely unprepared.

This same dynamic of actively teaching your kids must be applied with chores, with yard work, with learning how to fix things, with developing relationships. You must teach them. It takes selflessness to make your kids do stuff for themselves. When parents in today's world are so overwhelmingly busy with their own careers and social life and social media, they end up pacifying their children to make their own life easier. Suddenly, kids aren't taught even the basics of how to be an adult, of how to be a part of a family or community. At the slightest notion of work or chores, kids throw tantrums and parents compromise, making the moment easier, and the future much harder.

This is where the 40% rule can really help. It is a powerful tool parents have to help their kids tap into those reserves of perseverance and self-reliance. But you only get that by pushing your kids past the point of comfort. You only get that by teaching them humility and hard work.

TEACH YOUR KIDS TO SUFFER WELL

Jensen Huang, the CEO and founder of Nvidia, a leading tech corporation, recently spoke to students at Stanford University. While guest speakers are a regular feature at universities, Huang's comments to students made his speech quite memorable. "I wish you ample doses of pain and suffering," Huang told students. "Greatness is not intelligence. Greatness comes from character. And character isn't formed out of smart people, it's formed out of people who have suffered. Unfortunately, resilience matters in success. I don't know how to teach it to you except for I hope suffering happens to you."

Huang's message was one of unflinching truth. Unconventional compared to usual boilerplate speeches of working hard or staying positive, Huang emphasized that getting a top-rated education or the best internships are not predictors of success. Instead, he knows and has seen firsthand that resilience, grit, and determination make all the difference. These are what he looks for in job applicants; people with these traits lead to innovation and success.

Now, I'm not saying we must make our children unduly suffer, or become Navy SEALS, or never watch T.V. again. What I'm talking about is instilling a blue-collar mindset, a blue-collar soul into your kids. A soul of humility, of grit, of a tireless work ethic.

Parents have the absolute moral duty of teaching their kids to suffer well. That's not an idea, it's a habit. It's a disposition that's developed over time. So, parents ask yourself: when faced with suffering, can your kids tap into the extra reserves or not?

THE CODDLING CRISIS: A HISTORICAL PERSPECTIVE

To understand where we are, we need to look at where we've been. Post-World War II America saw a shift toward a more nurturing, child-centered approach to parenting. Dr. Benjamin Spock's 1946 book *The Common Sense Book of Baby and Child Care* encouraged parents to be more affectionate and responsive to their children's needs. While there are some, *some*, positive aspects to this emphasis, and while there were some, *some*, negative aspects to the pre-war authoritarian parenting, the net result is that we are in a mess today.

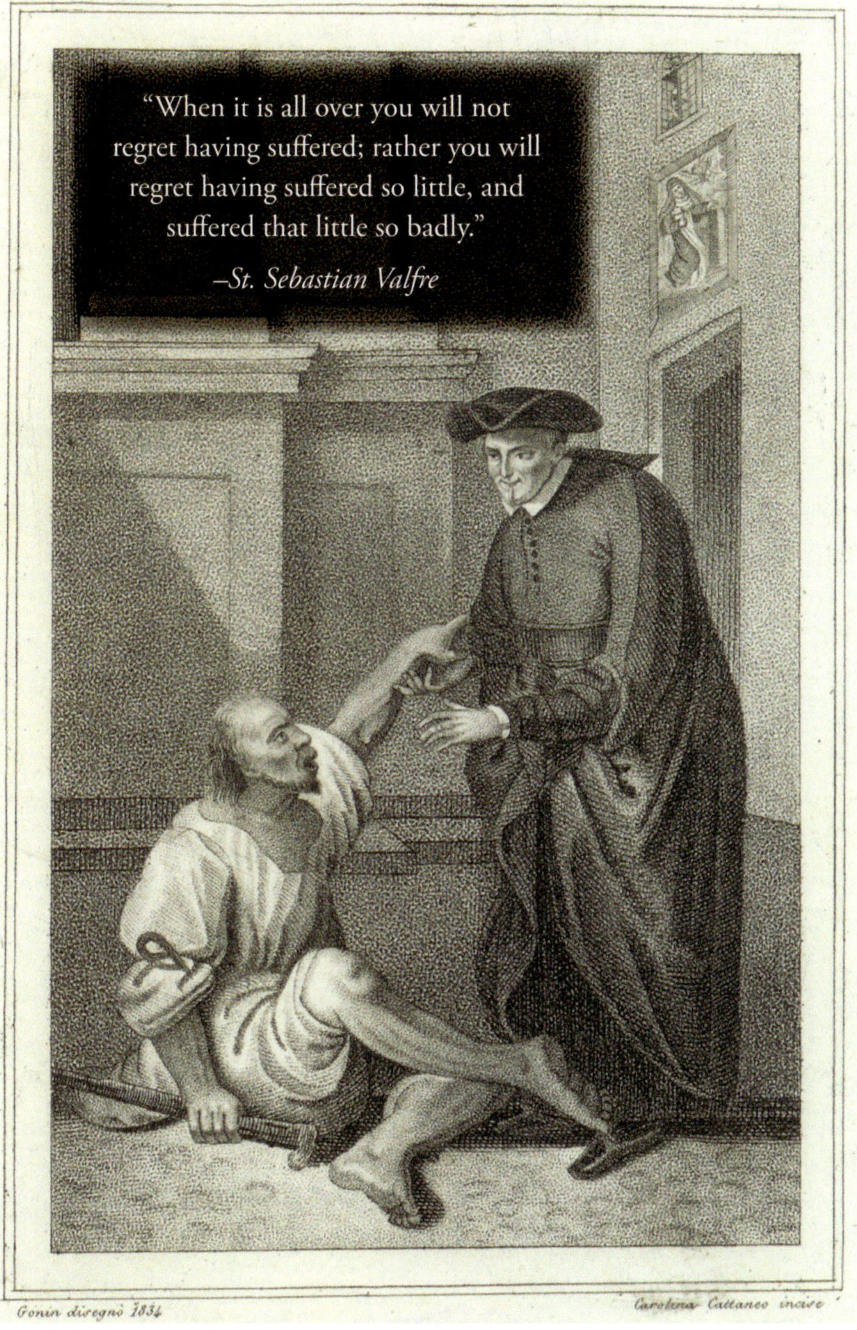
"When it is all over you will not regret having suffered; rather you will regret having suffered so little, and suffered that little so badly."
–St. Sebastian Valfre
Gonin disegnò 1834
Carolina Cattaneo incise

Fast forward to the 1980s and 1990s. Here we see the rise of the "helicopter parent." This term, coined by Dr. Haim Ginott, and popularized by Foster Cline and Jim Fay, described parents who hover over their children, ready to swoop in and solve any problem. The intentions were good—protect our kids, ensure their success—but the results? A generation of young adults who struggle with basic life skills and crumble at the first sign of adversity.

This reminds me of a funny incident years ago. We had friends over who had a two-year-old. We had a two-year-old son as well (we've had a two-year-old for over twenty years straight now). My son came up and asked Ashley, "Can I have a yogurt?" "Sure," she said, and then continued talking to our visitors. My son pulled a bar stool across the kitchen floor to the fridge, climbed up, opened the fridge, pulled out a yogurt cup, closed the door, climbed down, pulled off the top of the yogurt cup, threw the lid in the trash can, then pulled the bar stool across the floor again to the silverware drawer with one hand (holding the yogurt in the other), climbed up, opened the drawer, took out a spoon, put the spoon in the yogurt, closed the drawer, climbed down, pulled the stool back to the bar, climbed up the stool, sat at the bar, and ate his yogurt. Our friends thought my kid was a genius. They were flabbergasted. About halfway through the event they were gawking at the kid in amazement. They explained their kid couldn't do anything for himself.

I asked a weird question. "If you dropped dead in your house, leaving your two-year-old to fend for himself for a few days, would he starve to death or figure out how to get stuff out of the fridge, or how to open a banana, or how to get bread off the top shelf?"

"I guess he'd figure it out," my friend said.

"Exactly," I said. "The only difference between your kid and ours is that we force our kid to do stuff for himself. Given that he has a ton of other kids in the family and mom is often busy with a newborn, he often does stuff for himself just for expediency. But so long as you're pampering your kid, he's going to keep crapping his pants."

Admittedly, this might be a weird way of getting the point across, but I think it worked.

Folks, we also know moms who have groceries delivered to their college kids dorm rooms. I totally get that mom wants to take care of her little baby…but stop! This is delaying a very important part of human maturation. Humans for all of time have had to leave the cave and go hunt down food. Your spoiled little twenty-year-old baby doesn't even have to take a spear with him when he goes to the local Publix and sorts through the sushi selection and buys it with your ApplePay. For the love of all that is good, stop ordering his groceries. "But he doesn't have a car?" Well then, make him eat in the cafeteria. Or make him take the subway. Or an Uber. Or . . . now imagine them doing what you and I had to do in college . . . sucking up to an upper classman so he'd give you a ride to the store! That's right, even social skills of corroborating with others is being stifled by everyone living like an English Aristocrat with servants bringing food to them.

If you don't want your kid to starve to death one day, stop sending them food!

CHECK YOUR PRIVILEGE AT THE DOOR

Let's get real. If you're reading this, chances are you've got it pretty good. But that comfort you've worked so hard for? It's your child's kryptonite. A 2023 Harvard study found that nearly 1 in 3 young Americans latch onto their parent's employer, earning 17% more because of it. Sounds great, right? Wrong. This privilege is creating a generation of kids who can't handle adversity. Instead of forging their connection and blazing their own trails, these kids choose the path of least resistance. While it might give them a job in the short term, they become yet another helpless cog in the machine of comfort.

I was a child of great privilege. We lived in an upscale, white-collar neighborhood. There wasn't much opportunity to work with your hands or work with the land. And we really didn't do many chores. Most of that work was hired out. My parents, thank God, instilled so many wonderful principles in us, particularly the Faith, and they taught us hard work in other ways. But I'm not sure I ever fixed anything or built anything or cleaned anything until I was married.

When I got married, I began to see these activities as ends in themselves. If cutting the grass was just a means to the end of having a nice lawn, then once I had money there was zero reason to cut grass. But what if cutting grass was an end in itself? What if cutting wood and building a work bench or garden boxes was an end in itself? I wanted to learn a few things, and I did. And as time went on, I found that projects were extremely rewarding, particularly when done with the children. Mending a fence with your son is a marvelous event. And I've done just that.

Truth be known, I'm actually terrible at these things, but I've tried and gotten better. And my kids are better than me. I could easily afford a lawn service, but given that I have multiple teenagers, why would I deprive them of the great opportunity to build this little skill set, to encounter a sputtering small engine, to have to change oil and gas, or go with me to change the blades, and the pure joy of riding around and cutting grass. We'll talk more about rural life later on in this book. But suffice it to say, if you have privilege, check it at the door and go do stuff.

In short, parents, your overprotectiveness is crippling your children. A 2012 study published in the *Journal of Anxiety Disorders* found that overprotected children are more prone to worry and anxiety.[1] When parents constantly hover over their kid's shoulder, it instills the false worry in the kid that he's doing something wrong or that he's not capable or smart enough to be self-reliant. You're not just coddling them; you're setting them up for a lifetime of mental health issues. A 2022 study in *Frontiers in Psychology* linked overprotective parenting to higher occurrences of anxiety and depression in adult life.[2] Is that what you want for your kids?

SWEAT EQUITY: THE CURRENCY OF CHARACTER

Here's a wake-up call: chores aren't just about a clean house; they're about building character. A 20-year study published in the *Journal of Developmental and Behavioral Pediatrics* found that the best predictor of young adults' success in their mid-20s was whether they participated in household tasks at age 3 or 4.[3] The study found that when kids engage in activities that benefit the

---

1 Susanne Knappe et al, Characterizing the association between parenting and adolescent social phobia, *Journal of Anxiety Disorders*, vol. 26, Issue 5, 2012, 608-616.

2 Vigdal, Julia Schønning, and Kolbjørn Kallesten Brønnick. "A Systematic Review of "Helicopter Parenting" and Its Relationship With Anxiety and Depression." *Frontiers in psychology* vol. 13. 25 May. 2022.

3 White, Elizabeth M et al. "Associations Between Household Chores and Childhood Self-Competency." *Journal of developmental and behavioral pediatrics: JDBP* vol. 40 (2019): 176-182.

household and that require them to problem-solve or push themselves either mentally or physically, they develop a strong foundation of self-confidence and positive work-ethic. Yet, how many of us are robbing our kids of this crucial life lesson?

The American Academy of Child and Adolescent Psychiatry emphasizes that chores help children feel competent and responsible. They learn time management, organization, and the satisfaction of contributing to their family. But in our rush to ensure academic success, we're neglecting these fundamental life skills.

In my house, chores are a big deal. Our chore chart (*on the next page*) is like a heartbeat. Here, you can see how it works. Every night after dinner, I'm walking over to the chore chart and yelling (rather loudly) who has what chores. I expect them to get on it.

The more teenagers we have (right now our 7th child is 14, but the kids graduate from the chore chart at 18) the more difficult it is to get them to do their chores on time. They are gone. They have tons of activities. So, we have to ride them pretty hard. If they are going out to basketball practice or to hang out with friends, they *need* to knock out as much of their chore as possible. And if no one finishes it off by the time they have returned home, they have to do it, no matter how late. Imagine if I just let teenagers off the hook. They'd become spoiled very quickly. They have to contribute to this family, lest they think they are white-collar kids.

My kids haven't a clue about our financial resources. Why? Because I want them to never expect a handout. My two oldest kids, both married with a child, just purchased their own homes. It was amazing. Neither expected their mother and me to help in any way with a down payment. So, when we told them how we would like to contribute to their first home, they were totally surprised, extremely grateful, and both expressed hesitation to accept a financial gift. (It has been Ashley's and my long-term goal to help each kid purchase a home.) I was so proud of them. They ain't perfect, but they ain't spoiled—at all. We've raised them to expect little from others and a lot from themselves. And we are seeing the tremendous reward right before our eyes.

So don't be surprised that overprotective parenting is associated with low self-efficacy later in life. A 2014 study in the *Journal of Child and Family*

Daily Chores

SUNDAY	MONDAY	TUESDAY	WEDNESDAY
Peter	Jude	David	Imelda
Jude	Peter	Imelda	David
Paul	Teresa	Jude A.M. Paul P.M.	Annie
Teresa	Paul	Annie	Luke/ Thomas
Imelda	David	Peter	Paul

THURSDAY	FRIDAY	SATURDAY	Inside
Annie	Teresa	Paul	Dishes
Jude A.M. Paul P.M.	Paul	Teresa	Countertops
Imelda	Peter	Jude	Kitchen / Dining Room Floors
David	Jude	Peter	Rest of Downstairs
Jude	Luke/ Thomas	Imelda	Bonus Room Pick Up / Vacuum

Studies found that children of helicopter parents had lower scores on self-efficacy measures.[4] "Helicopter parenting can be particularly harmful during emerging adulthood when young adults are working toward developmental goals of self-reliance and autonomy," researchers found. "Whereas some parental protection of their children is a positive quality, helicopter parenting occurs in situations that do not warrant parental involvement. For example, a parent may contact their child's professor to dispute their child's low grade or contact a potential employer to negotiate their child's job offer and salary."

By constantly monitoring and protecting your children, you're sending a clear message: they're not capable of managing life by themselves. They're not capable of taking care of themselves, or saving money, or one day buying a home early in their marriage. Is that really the legacy you want to leave?

And by the way, don't you just love it when Ivy League-type studies prove to you what your common sense already knew? I cite many studies in this little book to show that even the crazy "experts" are seeing what you and I already know.

COMFORT IS THE ENEMY: EMBRACE THE STRUGGLE

Listen up, because this is crucial: your love for your children shouldn't be measured by how comfortable you make their lives but by how well you prepare them for life's challenges. What are your kids learning?

Dr. Angela Duckworth, author of *Grit: The Power of Passion and Perseverance*, argues that grit—a combination of passion and perseverance—is a better predictor of success than IQ or talent.[5]

When I first read this book, I looked throughout our sales organization and saw that the great salespeople came from a diverse background: some had been in sales for decades, some were from the ministry, some were farmers, including a former Amish fellow. Their personalities were likewise diverse: some were extraverted, others introverted; some were detail oriented, some were oblivious to details. But what was the one thing that all of them had in

---

4 Kouros, Chrystyna D et al. "Helicopter Parenting, Autonomy Support, and College Students' Mental Health and Well-being:" *Journal of child and family studies* vol. 26 (2017): 939-949.

5 Duckworth, Angela, *Grit: The Power of Passion and Perseverance* (New York: Scribner, 2016) 15-26.

common? Grit. The good ones all had a perseverance, a resilience, a courage. Grit is the perfect word. Just like my sales organization, your family is made up of radically different attributes. If you have two kids, you like to tell people they are opposites. Even with sixteen, I like to say they are all opposites (and then people have to think about that for a second). But what you, dear parent, can instill in your child's soul, no matter their God-given attributes, is grit. Grit: what a lovely word precisely because it is a little dirty. Such is life. And such can your child be, but only if you allow your kid to flex that muscle through discomfort and struggle.

"Work every day. No matter what has happened the day or night before, get up and bite on the nail."

–Ernest Hemingway

Haven't we all seen this in our friends, families, and colleagues? Is the smartest person really the most successful? In fact, I have said many times as an employer that the best thing that could happen to that guy or gal is to lose about 10 IQ points. Academic aptitude inflates people's ego faster than anything. They become elite in their minds. They move their soul into an Ivory Tower above everyone else. The one industry where this doesn't seem to hurt people too much is academics. But in the rest of the world, arrogance comes back around to bite you.

We spend way too much time as a nation praising our kids' academic achievements. Do me a favor: if you have a bumper sticker that says, "My kid is an Honor Roll student as Jefferson Middle School" please, I beg you, for the love of all that is good, rip the damn thing off. And then explain to your kid that their academics, while important, is not near the most important thing to be proud of. Would you have a bumper sticker that says, "My kid prays every morning before going to Jefferson Middle School" or "My kid sticks up for the fat kids at Jefferson Middle School" or "My kid is kind to nerds at Jefferson Middle School" or "My kid doesn't watch porn like the other kids as Jefferson Middle School." I don't think so. But each of these is 10X more important than his stupid GPA. Don't communicate the wrong message, mom and dad. If you advertise what you are proud of to every person on the road, it's going to reprioritize what your kid sees as important.

Speaking of middle school, your overprotectiveness can also make your children prime targets for bullying. A 2013 study published by BBC News found that overprotected children are more likely to experience bullying in school.[6] Why? Because you've infantilized them, denying them the chance to develop conflict management and self-defense skills. Is this how you protect them?

"Children need support but some parents try to buffer their children from all negative experiences," said Professor Dieter Wolke, lead researcher in the study. "In the process, they prevent their children from learning ways of dealing with bullies and make them more vulnerable."

He added: "It is as if children need to have some distress so that they know how to deal with conflict. If the parents all the time do it for them then the children don't have any coping strategies and are more likely targets."

When you as parents jump in to solve every problem, coddle every tantrum, fold to every demand, you take the vital moments of learning invaluable skills right out from under them. While these moments in raising children can be hard—especially with younger children—you must remember that giving into demands or coddling poor behavior only make it harder. Your job is to instill responsibility and self-efficacy. Your job is to raise self-assured kids who have grit and integrity. This can only happen if you lead by example and give your children the opportunity to learn these skills.

YOUR NEW PARENTING MANTRA: "FIGURE IT OUT"

Parents, it's time for a new approach. Instead of jumping in to solve every problem for your kids, start saying, "Figure it out." It's not cruel; it's an act of love. You're building problem-solving skills that will serve them for life.

---

6 Richardson, H., "Overprotected children 'more likely to be bullied.'" BBC News, April 26, 2013. https://www.bbc.com/news/education-22294974

Dr. Madeline Levine, psychologist and author of *The Price of Privilege*, warns that when parents routinely step in to prevent their children from failing, they interfere with the child's development of self-efficacy—the belief in one's ability to handle life's challenges.[7]

"Intrusion and support are two fundamentally different processes: support is about the needs of the child, intrusion is about the needs of the parent," Levine writes. "Children need work experiences to develop a sense that success is a function of their own efforts....We all want our children to put their best foot forward. But in childhood and adolescence, sometimes the best foot is the one that is stumbled on, providing an opportunity for the child to learn how to regain balance, and right himself."

Studies show that children of overprotective parents often engage in risk-taking behaviors later in life. They either become excessively fearful and timid, or wildly rebellious. Why? I think it's because they did not experience risk and reward enough early in life. It's as if that part of the brain doesn't work yet. Kids need to fail. Kids need to feel the pain of failure. It is the pain of failure that helps them make better risk assessments later in life.

I remember one day my sixteen-year-old son had a front headlight go out. He wanted to take it to the dealership. I told him not a chance. He had two options: 1) go to YouTube and figure it out, or 2) go to O'Reilly Auto Parts, talk to someone there, and figure out how to do this. It took him a few hours, but he did it. Sounds small. It is. Yet it is atomic. Even in a little lesson like this, it starts small but a huge atomic habit is built in which he learned to problem solve himself, to not be afraid of getting his hands dirty and stumbling through a learning process.

THE RIPPLE EFFECT: HOW YOUR PARENTING SHAPES SOCIETY

Parents, the stakes are higher than you might realize. We're not just raising kids; we're shaping the next generation of adults who will lead our communities, run our businesses, and govern our nation. The consequences of overprotective parenting extend far beyond your family.

7 Levine, Madeline, *The Price of Privilege* (New York: Harper, 2006).

A 2023 study by Gallup found that only 36% of U.S. employees are engaged in their work in 2020 and has dropped even lower since.[8] Could this be a result of a generation raised to expect constant guidance and praise, now struggling in workplaces that demand initiative and resilience? Could it be that they go from mommy and daddy telling them how special they are to the boss telling them how inadequate their work product is? As a nation, we are creating an economy of white-collar wimps.

Remember, every time you rescue your child from a challenge, you're stealing an opportunity for growth. Every time you solve a problem for them, you're robbing them of the chance to develop critical thinking skills. Every time you shield them from discomfort, you're weakening their ability to cope with life's inevitable hardships.

The choice is yours, parents. Will you continue to handicap your children with overprotection, or will you have the courage to step back and let them grow? The future of your children—and our society—depends on your answer. We need blue-collar mindsets more than we need technological revolution. We don't need faster microchips. We need workers who don't need safe places to scream and cry.

It's time to ditch the white-collar mindset and embrace the grit, resilience, and work ethic that will truly set our children up for success. It won't be easy, but then again, nothing worth doing ever is. Your kids are counting on you. Let's get to work.

---

8 Harter, B. J., "U.S. Employee Engagement Needs a Rebound in 2023". Gallup.com, January 25, 2023.